Unfailing

God's Assurance for Times of Change

Christopher M. Kennedy

CONCORDIA PUBLISHING HOUSE · SAINT LOUIS

This book is dedicated with love to my son Zachary. Zachary, you were an important change in my life. When your mom and I found out you were going to be born, I was struggling through a difficult season. Your name, Zachary, means "God remembers." I felt, and still feel, that your entry into my life was a clear sign from God that He remembers His people and never forgets us. You have brought so much joy into my life. You are a true gift from God. Your mom and I pray that you'll always remember God's love for you—in the ups and downs of life. We love you, and your Savior, Jesus, loves you most of all!

Published by Concordia Publishing House
3558 S. Jefferson Ave., St. Louis, MO 63118-3968
1-800-325-3040 • cph.org

Copyright © 2024 Christopher M. Kennedy

1   2   3   4   5   6   7   8   9   10   33   32   31   30   29   28   27   26   25   24

Praise for *Unfailing*

From our conception in our mother's womb until our last breath, we experience change. Our bodies change—they grow, they get injured, they grow old. Our relationships change as people come and go from our circle of friends and family. Life around us changes as society's values and norms transform—sometimes for the better, sometimes for the worse. Coping with change can be challenging to the most nimble and adaptable person among us. How do we find a way to survive the maelstrom of life's variations? From the pen of a skilled pastor comes *Unfailing: God's Assurance for Times of Change*. Pastor Christopher Kennedy presents a series of vignettes from the life of the Old Testament prophet Samuel, who experienced the momentous changes in Israel as it transitioned from a loose governance of divinely appointed judges to the reigns of its first kings, Saul and David. Through these moments from Samuel's life, Pastor Kennedy shows readers how God's servant Samuel adapted to a changing world. But more importantly, Kennedy demonstrates that Samuel's life points us toward an even greater person who is with us throughout every change in our lives and who is always available to guide us—Jesus, who is the same yesterday, today, and forever. Combining practical insights with solid biblical wisdom, *Unfailing* guides readers as they seek to navigate the changing currents in the stream of life.

ANDREW STEINMANN, DISTINGUISHED PROFESSOR EMERITUS OF
THEOLOGY AND HEBREW, CONCORDIA UNIVERSITY CHICAGO

If your life is anything like mine, the swirling pace of it all feels like it's accelerating. To keep the faith amid the rise of our world's rapid-fire stressors, we need teachers. Using Samuel—the prophet, priest, and king—as a primary model, Christopher Kennedy anchors us in Scripture, roots us in reality, and grounds us in the Spirit's practical wisdom. The promises of God on these pages are neither formulaic nor pie-in-the-sky. Rather, the concreteness of this book's applicability to the everyday challenges of everyday people will grace readers with truth that is timeless and, in truth, unfailing.

REV. JOHN ARTHUR NUNES, PHD; PASTOR, PILGRIM LUTHERAN CHURCH, SANTA
MONICA, CA; SENIOR FELLOW, CENTER FOR RELIGION, CULTURE, AND DEMOCRACY

Pastor Kennedy has blessed the church yet again with a relevant and deeply practical work that will help Christians navigate life in a fallen world. Kennedy's insightful and fresh examination of the prophet Samuel sharpens our understanding of one of the Bible's most overlooked characters and is brilliantly suited for helping us understand how to deal with change. Whether you are encountering Samuel's tumultuous story for the first time or simply getting reacquainted, you'll profit from this unique look at his life and times. In fact, I'm confident your encounter with this work will transform how you comprehend change in your own life. Instead of only lamenting changes with a "not again!" you'll learn how to better cope with and even grow stronger through the many curveballs life inevitably throws your way.

REV. DR. MICHAEL T. FIEBERKORN, ASSOCIATE PASTOR, ZION LUTHERAN CHURCH, ST. CHARLES, MO; AUTHOR OF *BATTLE OF THE SOUL: LUTHER REFORMS VICE AND VIRTUE*

Life moves on, and with it comes challenging changes. And when our increasingly non-Christian culture and bewildering digital technology pile on? We easily become depressed. Through personal reflection or small-group discussion, *Unfailing* is an opportunity to conquer change. Christopher Kennedy's look at changes in Samuel's life is creative. Most especially, I appreciate how he connects each change to our living Lord Jesus. "O Thou who changest not, abide with me!"

DALE A. MEYER, PRESIDENT EMERITUS, CONCORDIA SEMINARY, ST. LOUIS, MO

Contents

Foreword

The Old Testament is full of people chosen by God to accomplish His purposes. Some of them are considered heroes of the faith. Yet all of them were what Martin Luther called *simul justus et peccator*—at the same time both saint and sinner.

That simply means that along with the wonderful achievements these heroes were blessed by God to accomplish, they also manifested in their lives the same kinds of fickleness and failure that plague people today, including those who read this foreword and the one who wrote it.

For example, Adam willingly disobeyed God's simple command, succumbing to an invitation to do so by the woman who had been miraculously formed by God from Adam's own body. And then Adam blamed that woman, his beloved Eve, for his failure.

Noah was righteous in God's sight, chosen by God to survive the great flood and to preserve humanity and specimens of all other living creatures. Yet after surviving that horrendous ordeal, he got stupefyingly drunk and disrobed, shaming himself.

Abraham, Isaac, Jacob, Moses, Aaron . . . the list goes on of great Old Testament men of God with feet of clay. That list includes David, a mighty warrior-king.

David was the author of most of the psalms. A high-profile ancestor of Jesus. A man after God's own heart (1 Samuel 13:14). Yet he committed blatant adultery with Bathsheba, unsuccessfully tried to hide his participation in her pregnancy, and subsequently had her husband killed in battle.

And then there was Samuel. Chris Kennedy's selection of Samuel as the main character of the book you hold in your hand is intriguing.

Though a name recognizable to many, Samuel is not often the man who comes to mind when thinking about heroes of the Old Testament.

While Samuel's sons fell far short of being faithful descendants and children of God, Samuel himself was blessed to avoid the major blunders that befell many, if not most, of those chosen by God as prophet, priest, judge, king, or another significant biblical leader.

Samuel's life and ministry set the stage for the practical life applications today that you, the reader, will soon discover in the pages that follow.

Unfailing: God's Assurance for Times of Change is profound yet practical. Pastor Kennedy deftly describes the life and ministry of Samuel and also shares multiple examples of the life and ministry of Jesus. He skillfully uses those examples to provide inspirational guidance in circumstances of life people face today. People like you. People like me.

Throughout the pages of *Unfailing*, I found a clear and compelling communication of the life-changing power of the love of Jesus. And so will you.

This quotation from chapter 12 provides a powerful illustration and succinct summary:

> Through Jesus, a radical change takes place in us.
> Sinners become saints. Transgressors are transformed.
> Rascals are made righteous. The irredeemable are
> redeemed. Purchased by Christ's blood, you are what
> God declares you to be: a new creation in Christ!

Though this book is focused heavily on the life of Samuel, it's really about Jesus!

DR. GERALD B. "JERRY" KIESCHNICK
PRESIDENT EMERITUS, THE LUTHERAN CHURCH—MISSOURI SYNOD
CHIEF EXECUTIVE OFFICER, LEGACY DEO

Preface

This is a book about change, a prophet, a Savior, and you.

This is a book about change. All of us deal with change to some extent. For some people, change is invigorating. For others, it's unnerving. The kind of change we struggle with most is loss. Whenever we lose something that we value, we feel cheated. We feel lost. We struggle to accept the "new normal" and move forward.

God's Word is comprehensive in the variety of topics it addresses. In Scripture, we can find counsel for managing change in a godly way. God doesn't leave us to fend for ourselves in this broken and often confusing world. He comes to us by His Spirit and through His Word to help us navigate life.

This is a book about a prophet. The prophet's name is Samuel. You may be familiar with his life story, but I'd venture to say most Christians are not. As children in Sunday School, many of us learned about Samuel's calling from God in the night. Some may know that he anointed the first two kings of Israel. But beyond that, his story is largely unfamiliar to many believers.

Samuel, in fact, is a towering figure in the Bible. He's the only person in the Old Testament with two books named after him in our English Bibles—1 and 2 Samuel. Psalm 99:6 names Samuel along with Moses and Aaron as exalted priests. Jeremiah 15:1 names Samuel and Moses as men who stood before the Lord and spoke to Israel. Samuel was the last of the judges and the first of the prophets, as Peter highlighted in a sermon (Acts 3:24). And Samuel's name appears in the Hebrews 11 "Hall of Faith" (v. 32).

In our age of rapid change, Samuel is the perfect biblical figure to study. He lived in a time of great societal and personal change, as the following chapters will demonstrate. He demonstrated faith and leadership in those times. We also see the honesty of God's Word in showing us that Samuel, too, struggled with changes in his life.

This is a book about a Savior. Jesus said, "You search the Scriptures because you think that in them you have eternal life; and it is they that bear witness about Me" (John 5:39). All of the Bible—Old Testament and New Testament—points us to Jesus. In many ways, Samuel's life points us to Jesus. Only a few people in Israel's history occupied the threefold office of prophet, priest, and king or leader. The list is short, arguably as short as Moses, Samuel, and finally Jesus.

In many ways, Jesus is the "greater Samuel." Samuel spoke God's truth to the people; Jesus spoke the truth with a unique personal authority. Samuel offered sacrifices on behalf of the people; Jesus became the sacrifice on the cross for our sins. Samuel "judged" the people as their governing leader until anointing the first king; Jesus is King of kings and Lord of lords.

Looking to Jesus, we find the help that we need in the midst of loss, transition, and disorientation. As we struggle to make sense of life, He reorients us to His kingdom, His righteousness, and His eternal plan for us and all people.

This is a book about you. The pages of this book contain practical applications, stories, and other illustrations that I pray will provide insight and guidance as you walk with the Lord through the ups and downs of changes in your life.

CHRISTOPHER M. KENNEDY
SAN ANTONIO, TEXAS
JUNE 2023

PART 1

Change

A Fact of Life

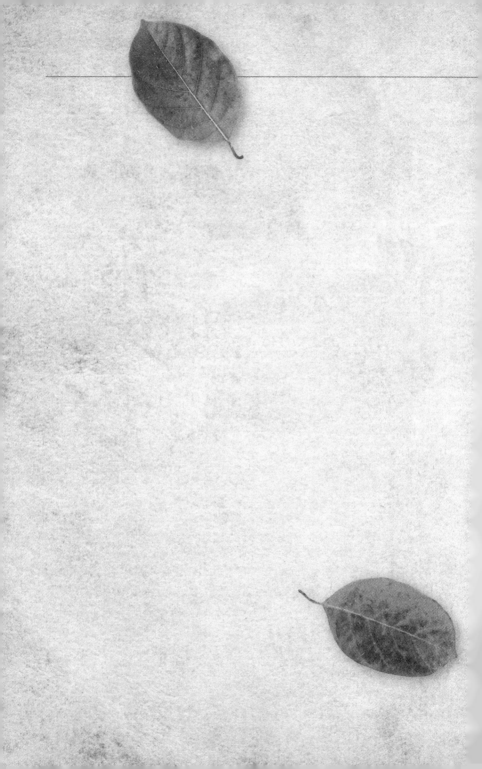

CHAPTER 1

A Strange New World

Steve Rogers wakes up and looks around. He's lying on a bed. Above him, a ceiling fan rotates slowly. Soft sunlight beams in from a slightly opened window. He hears a voice from a radio—a broadcast of a baseball game.

A woman enters the room. She greets him.

He asks her where he is. She answers that he's in a recovery room in New York City. He looks around and asks again, this time more forcefully, where he really is.

He stands and walks toward the woman, eyes burning with anger. She pushes a button, and two uniformed men enter through the door behind her.

In a flash of activity, the two men go flying through the wall, which is revealed to be part of a movie set. Rogers runs through a hallway. A door swings open as he bursts from the bottom floor of a skyscraper and into the daylight, right in the middle of Times Square.

He looks around in stunned bewilderment.

What is all of this? Fast-moving modern cars. People passing by in strange fashions. Towering video screens mounted on buildings. Sleek skyscrapers. It's all so futuristic, so foreign.

A man in a trench coat approaches him. He explains that the fake room was designed to ease him into twenty-first-century life.

After all, Rogers had been asleep for seventy years.

This is a scene from the 2011 movie *Captain America: The First Avenger*. Is it also a scene from your life? Not the action and adventure. But the sensation of going to sleep in one era and waking up in another.

The rapidly changing world around us might feel unrecognizable at times.

A World in Flux

I was born in 1982. In my lifetime, barely four decades, the world has changed dramatically.

When I was a child, my family used to go to Blockbuster to rent movies or video games. Blockbuster is now almost extinct, replaced by streaming services like Netflix.

If you were away from home, you brought quarters in case you needed to use a pay phone. Now we all carry cell phones.

My family used to subscribe to the daily print newspaper, as most families did. I remember eating breakfast with the sports page unfolded next to my cereal bowl. Today I get my news exclusively from news sites on my phone.

We shopped at the mall, Wal-Mart, or Target. Now e-commerce has asserted itself over brick-and-mortar stores.

I remember when we got a computer and had dial-up internet. Now anything less than high-speed fiber optic is regarded as unbearably sluggish.

These examples are mostly related to technology. We've also seen radical shifts in values and standards of behavior in recent decades.

My parents were born in the early 1950s. The world has changed even more for their generation. Many members of my congregation were born in the 1930s. That was before World War II. Before TVs were in every home. Before the internet. Before the interstate highway system. Before McDonald's, Burger King, or Chick-fil-A. And well before Starbucks.

Hard to Accept

It has been said that the only constants in life are death, taxes, and change. To many people, the rate of change in our world seems to be accelerating, and it can be a challenge to keep up. My grandmother spoke of the world as a merry-go-round moving faster and faster. Whenever she watched a news story that reinforced her conviction that society was spiraling out of control, like a child ready to dismount a ride, she'd say, "Stop the world! I want off!"

Virtually no area of life is exempt from change. Churches change as old members die or move away and new members join, bringing their own ideas and interests. Communities change—a farming community outside a major city morphs into a sea of subdivisions as the city expands outward. The workplace has been transformed as more people work remotely. Banking is different; many of us deposit checks electronically through our phones (and some rarely use checks at all). Change is all around us.

These changes can cause us to feel confused, unnerved, and homesick for a bygone era. You may be struck by a strong sense of displacement. Like Steve Rogers waking after seventy years and finding himself in the middle of modern-day Times Square, we can feel like strangers in an unfamiliar world.

In gathering information for this book, I surveyed my congregation and ministry colleagues about the topic of change. The first question was about societal changes: "In your lifetime, what changes in our world have been most difficult for you to accept?" Here are some of the answers:

- "The adversarial relationship of political parties. They don't just disagree—but seem to hate each other."
- "The amount of technology required to participate in many things."
- "The increasing cost of living."
- "Cell phones; continual connectivity."
- "The decrease in church attendance."
- "The renaming of schools and streets; taking down old statues commemorating the past."
- "Not knowing what to believe when watching or reading the news. Nowadays there is way too much fictitious, sensationalized, and persuasive journalism."
- "Overreach by the federal government in many aspects of our lives."
- "The loss of civility in everyday encounters."
- "The amount of norms that have been turned upside down."
- "Moving further from a biblical worldview."
- "The younger generations' growing shift toward more liberal ideologies."
- "The changing morals of sexuality and identity."
- "The speed at which we're expected to function—similar to the speed of machines, which is unsustainable as human beings."
- "Rapid increase in people who believe in conspiracy theories."
- "The increase in outward expressions of racism."
- "Mass shootings at schools are extremely difficult for me to accept. I lump this into the 'change' category because these shootings have altered our approach to and concept of safety."
- "Covid and the aftereffects."

It's a long list! Yes, a lot has changed and is changing.

The Biggest Changes Ever

While all these changes may feel drastic, the most radical change to ever rock humanity took place with our original parents, Adam and Eve. Picture the world in its original state. It was perfect. The Creator declared it all good, and so it was. Plants were sprouting. Trees were bearing fruit. Birds were flying, fish were swimming, land animals were crawling and galloping. God's beautiful creation sparkled with newness.

Then everything fell apart. In our day, we might say certain technologies are value-neutral, capable of being used for good or evil. The same was true of a piece of fruit from a tree in the middle of the Garden of Eden. When the fruit remained on the tree, as God instructed, all was good! But when that fruit became an instrument of rebellion against God, it became a tool for destruction.

And did it ever destroy! When Eve and then Adam fell for the serpent's temptation and ate the forbidden fruit, the world changed. The creation itself began to hemorrhage. From that point forward, thorns and thistles emerged from the earth, cutting the hands that cultivated the land and harvested its fruit. As the ultimate consequence, death entered the world.

Most tragically, relationships were torn asunder. A chasm of sin separated humanity from its Creator. Adam and Eve once walked with God in the garden. After the first sin, the man and woman hid from their loving Maker. Human relationships suffered too. Instead of loving and cherishing each other, man and woman began pointing fingers in blame.

How did God respond to this earth-shattering disaster? Did He sit by idly and let the curse of sin take over His world? No way! God enacted His plan of salvation, conceived "before the foundation of the world" (Ephesians 1:4). He announced that He would not let sin rule the day. Instead, He would rescue fallen humanity. He promised a Seed of the woman, who would crush the head of the tempter (Genesis 3:15). Then, "when the fullness of time had come, God sent forth His Son, born of a woman, born under the law, to redeem those who were under the law, so that we might receive adoption as sons" (Galatians 4:4–5). In Jesus, God disrupted the status quo of sin, death, and hell.

Everything changed for the good when "the Word became flesh and dwelt among us" (John 1:14). The incarnation of God's Son brought a new chapter into human history. Through His death on the cross, Jesus "abolished death and brought life and immortality to light through the gospel" (2 Timothy 1:10). That's an eternity-altering change! Then, three days later, Jesus rose, setting a new course for all who trust in Him. We are "born again to a living hope through the resurrection of Jesus Christ from the dead" (1 Peter 1:3).

Talk about change! Now we look forward to Christ's return, when everything will be transformed in the most wonderful way. A new heaven and a new earth await. And we will occupy these perfect places as people made new. "For the trumpet will sound, and the dead will be raised imperishable, and we shall be changed" (1 Corinthians 15:52). We will be changed—all for the better!

Samuel's Shifting Society

The prophet Samuel was well acquainted with change. During his lifetime, he experienced significant societal change. He grew up in the period of the judges. This was by no means a golden era for God's people. In many ways, it was just the opposite. For four centuries, from Joshua to Samuel, God's chosen people were stuck in a chaotic cycle. Enemy nations would oppress them, and God would raise up a leader, or judge, to rescue His people. Periods of peace lasting decades would ensue, followed by periods of subjugation. It was a roller coaster, a pattern that repeated itself over and over, as chronicled in the book of Judges.

The period of the judges was not ideal. It was, however, a familiar arrangement. It's what the people knew, what their parents knew, what their grandparents knew, and so forth.

Then the people demanded a king. Samuel resisted this societal change at first. In Israel's culture at the time, government and religion were tightly connected, so a change in one inevitably affected the other. When resistance proved futile, Samuel submitted himself to God's instruction to give the people what they demanded: a king. The transition from judges to kings was rocky, especially when the first king, Saul, strayed from God's will.

Societal changes are challenging in their own ways. They affect us, but to some extent, we can keep societal changes at arm's length. Their impact is dispersed among many people. Personal changes, however, have a specific impact on us individually and as families. These relate most directly to our loved ones and sometimes our very personhood. These changes can require tremendous inner resources as we seek to adapt. Chapter 2 takes a closer look at the changes that hit closest to home.

FOR DISCUSSION

1. What do you hope to get out of your study of this book?

2. What have been the biggest societal changes in your lifetime?

3. Of the societal changes noted on the survey, which one has affected you the most?

4. Think about the comments from the survey. Are there any that differ from your experience? If so, which one(s)? Why?

5. Considering how much the world has changed, especially in recent decades, what are your hopes and concerns for the next generation?

6. Read Genesis 3:8–19. What changes happened after the first sin?

7. Based on this chapter and your own knowledge, what changes did Jesus accomplish through His life, death, and resurrection?

8. Christ's return will bring the ultimate change for all creation. What are you looking forward to most about Christ's return? Is there anything about His return that causes concern?

CHAPTER 2

Changes That Hit Close to Home

"I don't like change. I've had so many changes in my life. I don't want any more."

I've heard these words on multiple occasions from Sonja, a dear member of the congregation I pastor. Born in 1932 in eastern Germany, Sonja grew up in affluence. Her family lived in a stately eight-bedroom home with east and west wings. During World War II, she and her family had to flee their home. They were refugees living in cramped quarters in western Germany. Life was never the same after that. Her family lost nearly everything in the war, including the house and all the furniture in it. Life had been turned upside down.

No wonder Sonja is change-averse. She likes her worship to stay the same. She wants to live in her house as long as possible, into her nineties. Losses are particularly hard as friends grow old and die. Because she has lost all of her immediate family and many friends, Sonja tells me she sometimes feels like a leftover. I tell her she's not a leftover—she's the strong one, the last one standing!

If only the good things in life could be frozen in place, unalterable. You and I know it can't be that way. As long as the world continues turning, change happens.

Societal changes can have a great impact on us. But to some extent, those changes form an outer layer around us. The inner layer consists of personal changes: marriage, divorce, the birth of a child, illness, moving to a new home, the death of a loved one, and more. Every generation of Adam and Eve's children has been affected by significant personal changes—changes that strike at the core of our being. Many of them are good—marriage and the birth of children are among life's most joyful moments. Yet even the good changes add some stress to our lives and bring numerous accompanying changes.

Disruptors

In his book *Life Is in the Transitions: Mastering Change at Any Time*, author and researcher Bruce Feiler describes major life changes as disruptors. Based on a compilation of data about jobs, moves, accidents, health issues, and more, Feiler estimates that the average adult faces between thirty and forty disruptors in a lifetime.[1] If you live to be eighty years old, that means you'll encounter a major life change about once every two years.

Furthermore, Feiler has a term for extreme personal changes, the kind that completely upend our lives: lifequake. A lifequake can be personal—a career change, a cancer diagnosis, foreclosure on your home—or it can be collective, like a war or a natural disaster. He estimates that the average adult endures anywhere from three to five lifequakes over a lifetime.[2]

In chapter 3 of my book *Equipped: The Armor of God for Everyday Struggles*, I describe a tool called the Social Readjustment Rating

---

1   See Bruce Feiler, *Life Is in the Transitions: Mastering Change at Any Age* (New York: Penguin Press, 2020), 71.
2   See Feiler, *Life Is in the Transitions*, 79.

Scale. It was developed in 1967 by two psychiatrists and assigns a point value to different life events. The more stress an event places on a person, the higher the number. Death of a spouse heads the list with one hundred points. The next four are divorce, marital separation, jail time, and the death of a close family member.

Some good things make the list. Marriage is seventh. Retirement is tenth. Pregnancy is twelfth. These good things can be stressful. Husbands and wives, you know that your spouse can be a challenge! Retirement can bring greater freedom of schedule, but it also can result in a loss of purpose. Or maybe you didn't want to retire but were forced out. Pregnancy is exciting and nerve-racking at the same time. Some pregnancies are filled with complications that put a tremendous strain on expectant mothers and fathers.

Some life changes can't be scheduled. Deaths happen when they happen and are always an intrusion. Likewise, you don't schedule colliding with another car or inadvertently stepping off a curb, falling, and breaking a bone. No doubt, you know from personal experience the upheaval that unexpected changes bring.

In the congregational survey, I asked, "In your lifetime, what personal changes have been most difficult for you to accept?" The most frequent answers given were health issues, aging, and loss of loved ones. Here are some of the responses:

- "The onslaught of health challenges as I age."
- "Divorce."
- "Dealing with the loss of my son."
- "Blindness."
- "A parent's deepening dementia from Alzheimer's and Parkinson's diseases."
- "Loss of spouse."
- "Relocating to a different part of the country."

- "Cancer diagnosis."

- "Friends turning on me."

- "Infertility."

- "Going from 'normal' to 'disabled.'"

- "Children leaving home."

- "Family moving to heaven."

- "Moving away from friends and family."

- "Addition of children to the family."

- "Death of loved ones and why they are taken too soon."

- "Unwanted job changes."

- "How my daughter has been negatively affected by the attitudes and actions of her friends, pulling her away from the values of our family."

- "The death of one parent and the aging of another parent."

- "Physical and mental deterioration. Lost dreams because of the needs of daily circumstance."

- "Taking on a new challenge of becoming a single woman in the later stage of my life."

- "Getting older! Specifically, turning sixty and realizing I'm not immortal!"

- "Watching grandparents grow old and lose independence."

- "Empty nest; retirement."

While some changes can't be scheduled, other changes are more within our control. When possible, it's advisable to avoid making a bunch of changes at the same time. It can be unwise to get married, buy a new house, begin an advanced degree program, and change jobs . . . all in the same month! God designed our bodies as systems with limits. When it comes to personal changes, pacing is prudent.

But sometimes changes simply cluster together. My wife, Ashley, and I had our first child, Caleb, when I was thirty. Then, almost every other year, God blessed us with our three other children: Ethan, Emma, and Zachary. Those were joyful years! They also were challenging years. During those years, our church's longtime senior pastor was transitioning to retirement, and he had mentored me as his successor. After becoming senior pastor, I worked with congregational leadership on a comprehensive vision for our church, which resulted in a new building on our campus and a daughter church in the rapidly growing western outskirts of San Antonio. These were exciting ventures—and a lot at once.

All of these things were, in essence, good! Cumulatively, they added up to a lot of change at one time, personally and professionally. By His grace, God sustained me and gave me the energy I needed during that busy season.

You may be in a season of change right now. Perhaps all of the changes are necessary and timely. Or maybe you have some flexibility to defer some events to a time in life with fewer changes.

Changes in Jesus' Life

When Jesus Christ became man, He experienced a variety of personal changes, some painfully difficult. He took on our human nature—and everything a human life entails—so He could conquer sin, death, and hell for all people. Consider some of these personal changes He faced throughout His life:

His role changed. Jesus' Baptism inaugurated His public ministry. Before His Baptism, Jesus was a private citizen, so to speak. After His Baptism, Jesus was a public figure, a rabbi. From that point forward, He had students—the twelve disciples. He had an audience as He taught and performed miracles. As Jesus' fame grew, He lost any semblance of anonymity. Crowds followed Him. He also had enemies, as opposition formed against Him. As Jesus Himself said, "Whoever is not with Me is against Me" (Luke 11:23).

His location changed. As a young child, His family moved from Bethlehem to Egypt to Nazareth. During His Galilean ministry, His home base was Capernaum, along the Sea of Galilee. But Jesus didn't have a permanent address. He was constantly changing locations, packing up His luggage and traveling to a new place, dependent on others for lodging. Once, Jesus said, "Foxes have holes, and birds of the air have nests, but the Son of Man has nowhere to lay His head" (Luke 9:58).

His relationships changed. He lost friends because of death. When Jesus found out that John the Baptist had been beheaded, it appears that our Savior was profoundly affected and needed to process the news in a solitary place (see Matthew 14:13). People once loyal turned their backs on Jesus. His family called Him crazy; the Gospel of Mark records that "when His family heard [that Jesus had gathered followers], they went out to seize Him, for they were saying, 'He is out of His mind'" (3:21). During Holy Week, crowds of His supporters cheered Him on Palm Sunday. A few days later, crowds of His enemies condemned Him as a criminal. His closest companions became unreliable: one disciple betrayed Him with a kiss, another disciple three times denied knowing Him, and the rest of the disciples fled.

The Word became flesh, enduring all kinds of painful changes. We have a High Priest who sympathizes with us in our weaknesses (Hebrews 4:15). Just as we struggle through losses and life's other disruptions, Jesus also experienced these hardships. He accepted the troubles that come with being human.

After suffering for our sins by dying on the cross, He experienced one more change: His resurrection. He went from dead to alive! What a stunning transformation!

Changes in Samuel's Life

Samuel also experienced a number of life changes, chronicled in the pages ahead. He went from learning under the priest Eli to being called by God and given an intimidating first assignment: prophesy against Eli and his sons. Over time, Samuel's role expanded; he went from being an informal leader to being the judge, or the divinely appointed deliverer-leader, over Israel. That's a lot of responsibility and a major shift in identity!

And just as surely as Samuel ascended in leadership, he also had to step back. When Saul became king, Samuel had to relinquish some authority, which now belonged to the king. Samuel remained the prophet and priest of Israel, but governmental leadership now fell under the king. As Samuel grew old, he transitioned out of ministry altogether. These were not easy changes.

The Bible teaches us to have faith in the God of our salvation. Through the events of Samuel's life, we'll see the importance of trusting in God, especially when life is shifting and we're trying to keep our bearings. God was with Samuel, guiding the prophet through his life changes. In His faithfulness, God leads us by His Holy Spirit in seasons of transition.

FOR DISCUSSION

1. Are you generally invigorated by change? Or do you tend to view change as an unwelcome intrusion?

2. On the list of difficult personal changes, which can you relate to most?

3. Share some disruptors you've experienced in recent years.

4. If you're comfortable sharing, what events in your life would you consider lifequakes?

5. Tell about a good change that nevertheless added stress to your life.

6. Have you experienced a season of many changes clustered together? Please share.

7. Jesus underwent changes in His roles, locations, and relationships. Which of those three has been a bigger area of change for you?

8. Mark 3:21 reveals that Jesus' family thought He was crazy. How would you feel if your family formed such an opinion of you?

9. Hebrews 4:15 teaches that Jesus sympathizes with us in our weaknesses. Talk about what that means to you.

CHAPTER 3

What the Bible Says about Change

For everything there is a season, and a time
for every matter under heaven.

ECCLESIASTES 3:1

In the beginning, God maintained the status quo."

Of course, that's not what Genesis 1:1 says! No, the Bible's first verse describes change. "In the beginning, God created the heavens and the earth." Formerly, only God existed. Then God introduced change by making the universe, including our planet and everything in it.

"Behold, I am keeping all things the way they are."

That's not how the Bible ends either. No, the Bible begins with change and ends with change. In the penultimate chapter of the Bible, God declares, "Behold, I am making all things new" (Revelation 21:5). This broken world will not remain as it is. Christ will return, bringing with Him a new heaven and a new earth.

The Bible is all about change. God created all things good. Then Adam and Eve fell into sin, tragically altering the relationship between the Creator and His creation. When God sent Jesus into the world, a wonderful reversal happened! By dying for our sins and rising in victory, Jesus reconciled us to God. Salvation itself is change!

Change is part of life, including our life with God. With the Holy Spirit's help, we *grow* in faith—we don't stay the same. Through study and reflection, we gain a more mature understanding of His Word. Fittingly, the Bible provides many insights about change. As we prepare to study Samuel and the transitions of his lifetime, let's first explore the Bible's teachings about change.

God's Immutability

The Bible clearly states that God does not change. Change happens within the universe He created, but God stands outside of creation. He is completely sufficient in every way. God is perfect. Nothing about Him could be improved upon, so He stays the way He is. This is the doctrine of immutability.

Contrasting the transiency of the heavens and the earth with the permanence of God, the psalmist wrote, "They will perish, but You will remain; they will all wear out like a garment. You will change them like a robe, and they will pass away, but You are the same, and Your years have no end" (Psalm 102:26–27).

God's unchanging nature is good news! He is always loving. "His steadfast love endures forever" (Psalm 136:1). He is always merciful, always kind, always forgiving. You can always count on God for these things.

How reassuring it is to know that these qualities of God are consistent and reliable! Perhaps you've experienced the opposite with people. Maybe someone who once was a trusted friend was very positive but became more critical and irritable over time. Or maybe you've been in a relationship that started out strong, but both of you changed over time and drifted apart. One day at the gym, I ran into a former neighbor. He candidly shared with me struggles in his marriage, confiding sadly, "She's not the same person I married." Sometimes people change so much that they seem like totally different people. It can feel confusing as we seek to understand and love them.

People change, many times for better, but sometimes for worse. God doesn't change. He's the Alpha and the Omega, perfect from one end of eternity to the other.

God doesn't change, nor does His commitment to His people. He makes and keeps covenants. He proves Himself faithful over and over. In the last book of the Old Testament, God says, "For I the LORD do not change; therefore you, O children of Jacob, are not consumed" (Malachi 3:6). At that time, the children of Jacob, the faithful remnant, had endured tremendous upheaval. They were exiled to a foreign land and returned decades later to the rubble of past glory. But they still had reason for hope. Circumstances were disheartening, but God was by their side to sustain them.

Likewise, God promises to be your steady rock when your world is in flux. He continues to supply us with all we need out of His boundless goodness. "Every good gift and every perfect gift is from above, coming down from the Father of lights, with whom there is no variation or shadow due to change" (James 1:17).

Our Mutability

The Bible clearly presents God as unchanging—and that's a reason for comfort! By contrast, the Bible points out repeatedly the mutability, or changing nature, of humanity.

Change is a fact of life for mortal beings in physical bodies. In 2 Corinthians 4:16, Paul writes that "our outer self is wasting away." As we age, the "wasting away" becomes more and more pronounced. Our bodies change. Gravity messes up our physique. We wrinkle. We develop issues with blood pressure. Like a vehicle with high mileage, our parts wear out and need replacement—hips, knees, shoulders. One church member complained to her doctor about nagging back pain. The doctor said he could give her medication to minimize the pain but not to eliminate it. "You can't die of a bad back," he told her playfully.

Physical deterioration is one sign of our mutability, our propensity to change. It's also true that our circumstances change. Families grow with births and marriages, and families shrink with deaths and divorces. We leave one job and begin a new one. Our bank account fluctuates as funds come in and go out (and usually it's too much going out!). Wonderful neighbors move away, and rowdy neighbors move in, or the opposite—the noisy neighbors finally leave, and much quieter residents take their place!

Few people have experienced circumstances rising and falling and rising again like Job did. You may know his story. As his book begins, his life is filled with gifts from above: a wife, ten children, property, animals, one party after another, good health, and a vibrant faith life. What more could a person ask for?

Then the bottom fell out. Job lost his children, his animals, his house, his health. It all changed for the worse.

Fast-forward to the end of the book of Job. After processing his losses with a group of mostly unhelpful friends, Job's fortunes are restored twofold. Job had everything, lost everything, and gained everything again.

Throughout the book of Job, we see Job struggle with the losses—the changes he never wanted to happen. His initial reaction is inspiring: "The LORD gave, and the LORD has taken away; blessed be the name of the LORD" (Job 1:21). In other words, whether changes in life thrill us or depress us, God's essential nature doesn't change, and our reason for praising Him remains.

Job's story points ahead to a greater story of shifting circumstances. Before His incarnation, Jesus in His heavenly glory had everything— beyond what we can imagine. For our sakes, He willingly lowered Himself. No one lost more than God's Son when He took on human flesh. In Mary's womb, the infinite became finite.

His descent continued. He became a servant, washing His disciples' feet, eating with sinners and tax collectors, touching lepers to heal them. Then He lowered Himself as far as He could go. "And being found in human form, He humbled Himself by becoming obedient to the point of death, even death on a cross" (Philippians 2:8). After His final breath, He was lowered from the cross and entombed.

Then, on the third day, things changed . . . and did they ever! Jesus rose from death. He walked out of the grave. After showing others that He was alive, He ascended back into heaven, where He returned as a conquering hero and regained His throne.

Because Jesus' circumstances changed from death to life, your circumstances also changed from death to life. Though your outer self is wasting away, your "inner self is being renewed day by day" (2 Corinthians 4:16). Baptized into His name, you are freed from the curse of sin and bound for heaven. Eternity awaits! Resurrection awaits! In Christ, change is here and change is coming, and it's all for the good!

Seasons

To help us understand the nature of change, the Bible speaks of seasons. Things come, and things go. It's the nature of life on earth.

In Ecclesiastes, the preacher (presumably Solomon) wrote, "For everything there is a season, and a time for every matter under heaven" (3:1). Ecclesiastes 3 goes on to list some of these seasons of life:

"A time to be born, and a time to die" (v. 2). Few events alter our world more than births and deaths. First-time parents find out quickly that life will never be the same again. Conversely, when we lose a loved one who was integral to our life—a parent, a spouse, a child—we discover that life won't be the same, and it's excruciating.

"A time to break down, and a time to build up" (v. 3). Sometimes things grow—businesses, churches, investments. But nothing can stay on an upward trajectory forever. As there are seasons of growth, or building up, there also are seasons of decline, or breaking down.

"A time to keep, and a time to cast away" (v. 6). Have you ever had trouble getting rid of things? Attics, basements, garages, and spare bedrooms become repositories of items we no longer need but just can't bear to part with. A church member told me about the time he and his wife moved to a new house. They had boxes at the old house that had been untouched for fifteen years. They debated whether they really needed to transfer those boxes to the new house just so they could sit unopened for another fifteen-plus years! There's a time to keep and a time to cast away. Garage sale!

Life is filled with seasons. We cause ourselves and others a lot of heartache when we fail to recognize the present season. We find ourselves fighting against reality—holding on when it's time to let go, speeding up when it's time to slow down, taking risks when it's time to play it safe, expecting peace and quiet when the house is filled with young children. Seasons are a part of life. Acknowledge the season and do your best to live within it.

In the Old Testament, Joseph understood the principle of living within the season. As second-in-command of Egypt, he had to match government programs with the opportunities and needs he perceived. During seven years of abundance, he stockpiled grain. Then a famine decimated the land, and things changed. The season of gathering ended. The season of distribution began. Joseph matched his actions to the season, and the people under his care benefited—and survived.

How are you at acknowledging the seasons? Do you fight against change with all your might? Or do you seek to adapt, to find new ways to thrive?

Seasons in Jesus' Life

Jesus, the Son of God, is the same yesterday, today, and forever. But in His human nature, Jesus, the Son of Mary, knew every season of life that we know, from childhood through adulthood to death and beyond—His glorious resurrection. In each season, He excelled with perfect obedience to His heavenly Father and perfect love toward humanity.

In the season of His youth, Jesus was focused on His heavenly Father. After the infancy narratives, we have only one story from Jesus' childhood. It's when His parents were traveling from Jerusalem to their home in Nazareth and realized Jesus was missing! It was a parent's nightmare—losing a child. To their relief, Jesus was safe in the temple. He stayed behind in His Father's house, astounding His audience with His knowledge and insight. Devotion to His heavenly Father came first for Jesus.

In a season of transition, Jesus was humble. At age 30, Jesus began His public ministry. When Jesus approached John the Baptist to be baptized, John objected. But Jesus insisted, saying, "Let it be so now, for thus it is fitting for us to fulfill all righteousness" (Matthew 3:15). He entered the water, standing in the place of sinners, just as He would later stand in the place of sinners on the cross.

In a season of building, Jesus was decisive and purposeful. He recruited His disciples, calling them out of their regular vocations. He invited them to become fishers of men and to take up their crosses and follow Him. He trained them and sent them out for mission work. He prepared them for the day when He would not be with them.

In a season of popularity, Jesus leveraged His platform to proclaim the nearness of God's kingdom. He spoke before thousands, amazing them with His authoritative teaching. He performed miracles, or signs, to point to Himself as the way, and the truth, and the life.

In a season of growing opposition, Jesus was undeterred. The teachers of the law and the chief priests were desperately grasping for ways to expose Him as a phony. They played Stump the Rabbi with Jesus, but He always outsmarted them with wisdom from above.

In a day of suffering, Jesus submitted Himself unto death. He endured mockery, spitting, slapping, nailing, indescribable pain. "He humbled Himself by becoming obedient to the point of death, even death on a cross" (Philippians 2:8).

In a moment of holy vindication, Jesus was triumphant. Risen from the grave, for forty days He showed Himself alive to more than five hundred people. He reinstated a fallen disciple, Peter. He gave the Great Commission—to make disciples of all nations. He taught. He blessed. And then He ascended, ushering in the season of the church, a season that will last until He returns in final glory.

God Is in Control

Some seasons in Jesus' life were more difficult than others. For us, some seasons are enjoyable, filled with happiness. Others come with struggles marked by sadness and confusion.

A single change, or a series of changes, can bring us into a new season of life. In most cases, we don't decide when a season begins or ends. Changes can be a frustrating reminder that we don't control every factor of our lives. At the same time, changes remind us who is in control: God.

In seasons of change, people in the Bible learned who was really in control. Daniel experienced how changes can make us feel powerless. Daniel's world was turned upside down when he was deported to Babylon after the fall of Jerusalem. Yet he remembered who was really in charge. Daniel declared, "Blessed be the name of God forever and ever, to whom belong wisdom and might. He changes times and seasons; He removes kings and sets up kings" (Daniel 2:20–21).

Think about Moses. An adopted son of Pharaoh's daughter, Moses killed an abusive Egyptian slave-master and fled into the wilderness. For forty years as a shepherd in the desert, he may have felt demoted from royalty to renegade. Yet God was working out His plan. He called Moses from the burning bush and told him, "Come, I will send you to Pharaoh that you may bring My people, the children of Israel, out of Egypt" (Exodus 3:10).

Then there's Esther. The opposite of Moses, she was promoted from commoner to royalty. As queen, she experienced new pressures and expectations. Those pressures intensified when her uncle, Mordecai, alerted her to a scheme to exterminate the Jews. Mordecai said, "And who knows whether you have not come to the kingdom for such a time as this?" (Esther 4:14). God had positioned her for that exact moment.

And then there's Samuel. Many things in his life were beyond his control. He was born during the tumultuous period of the judges, when the people had forsaken God's laws and elevated their own desires as supreme. As a boy, Samuel didn't apply for a job as a prophet; God called Samuel and gave him vital messages to communicate to Israel. The people demanded a king—not what Samuel had in mind for them. Instead of looking to God's prophet as their leader, a truly unique arrangement, they wanted to be just like all the other nations with a king leading them into battle. To Samuel's disappointment, the people got what they demanded. Samuel's role changed. But God's role didn't. The Lord was sovereign over the events of Samuel's life—dramatic events, pivotal events.

And to those events we now turn our attention.

FOR DISCUSSION

1. When is change good?

2. The Bible teaches that God doesn't change. How is this truth comforting for you?

3. Put yourself in Job's shoes. If you lost everything, how would that affect your view of God?

4. Read 2 Corinthians 4:16. What does Paul mean by "outer self" and "inner self"? How is the inner self "renewed day by day"?

5. Read Ecclesiastes 3:1–8. Choose one of the pairings of opposites and explain why it resonates with you.

6. Life is filled with seasons. How would you characterize the season you're in right now?

7. Recall the story of Joseph, referenced in this chapter and described in detail in Genesis 41. How did he match his efforts to the season? How can you match your actions to the season of life you're in?

8. This chapter gave several examples of biblical figures who experienced significant change: Daniel, Moses, Esther, and Samuel. Of the first three people (since we'll cover Samuel throughout the book), which person's situation do you relate to most closely?

PART 2

The Life of Samuel

Eli is high priest/judge	1109–1069 BC
Samuel is born	ca. 1090 BC
God calls Samuel in the night	ca. 1073 BC
The ark of the covenant is returned to Israel	1068 BC
Samuel is judge	1060–1049 BC
Samuel anoints Saul as king	1049 BC
Samuel confronts Saul	ca. 1020 BC
Samuel anoints David as king	ca. 1019 BC
Samuel dies	ca. 1012 BC

Dates come from Andrew E. Steinmann, *1 Samuel*, Concordia Commentary (St. Louis: Concordia Publishing House, 2016), 22, 52, 113, 182, 290.

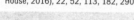

Samuel

God's Man for a Time
of Transition

CHAPTER 4

Change Is Coming

(1 SAMUEL 1)

For this child I prayed, and the LORD has granted me my petition that I made to Him.

1 SAMUEL 1:27

Something has to change!"

Have you ever spoken or thought those words?

A man goes to the doctor and gets a bad report. He's a walking time bomb, a heart attack waiting to happen. Overweight. Smoker. High blood pressure. High cholesterol. If he wants to live long enough to see his grandchildren, the doctor insists, the man needs to commit to some major lifestyle adjustments. Something has to change!

A college student has been staying up late partying and then sleeping through classes. As a result, her grades are plummeting. She had a scholarship, but she's going to lose it if she doesn't pass her classes. If she wants to complete college, she needs to get serious about school. Something has to change!

A couple's marriage is on the verge of collapse. Every day brings a new argument, a new set of frustrations, a louder shouting match than the day before. They can't agree on anything. He belittles her.

She insults his intelligence. If they want to preserve their marriage, they have to stop fighting and start getting along. Something has to change!

In some cases, we might say, "I don't like changes." But what we really mean is, "I don't like changes that have a negative impact on me." We're in favor of some changes. Politicians have won elections by tapping into constituents' longings with slogans like "Change you can believe in." People want changes that have a positive impact on them. A pay raise is a change. Moving into a new house better suited for your family's needs is a change. After years of being single and lonely, having a charming date for Valentine's Day is a change.

Not all change is bad. When life is hard, we find ourselves longing for good changes.

Judges

Samuel was born in an era desperately needing change. His story follows on the heels of the book of Judges. In fact, Samuel is so closely connected with the book of Judges that Jewish tradition names him as its author.[3]

The book of Judges describes the period between Joshua and Samuel. The book covers about two hundred years of Israel's history, from 1250 to 1050 BC.[4] This period was tumultuous for God's people. Over and over, they fell away from the Lord. This refrain appears repeatedly: "The people of Israel did what was evil in the sight of the LORD" (Judges 2:11; 3:7, 12; 4:1; 6:1; 10:6; 13:1). They served other gods. As punishment, God gave the Israelites into enemy hands—the Moabites enslaved them for eighteen years, the Canaanites oppressed them for twenty years, the Midianites for seven years, the Philistines

---

3   See Andrew E. Hill and John H. Walton, *A Survey of the Old Testament*, second ed. (Grand Rapids, MI: Zondervan, 2000), 192.

4   See Horace D. Hummel, *The Word Becoming Flesh: An Introduction to the Origin, Purpose, and Meaning of the Old Testament* (St. Louis: Concordia Publishing House, 1979), 113.

and Ammonites for eighteen years, and the Philistines again for forty years (see Judges 3:14; 4:3; 6:1; 10:7–8; 13:1). Along with being oppressed by these nations, God's people self-destructed through infighting. At one point, the tribe of Benjamin went to war with the other eleven tribes.

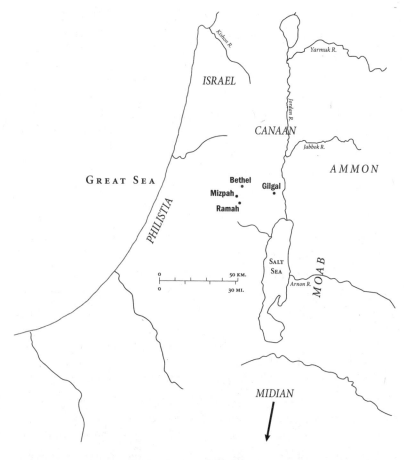

These were turbulent years for Israel. The concluding words of the book of Judges identify the root issue: "Everyone did what was right in his own eyes" (Judges 21:25). Instead of conforming their behavior to God's expectations, everyone did what they wanted, what suited their needs, what felt good in the moment. These were the first postmoderns! The truth didn't matter—only *my* truth.

Regardless of how far His people strayed, God remained faithful. Even when they pushed Him away, God continued to pursue them. He provided judges. These were not courtroom judges who presided over a trial. These men and women called judges were divinely appointed leaders raised up to deliver God's people and to reestablish order. They were called judges, one scholar explains, because they were charged with "maintaining justice by means of righteous judgments."[5]

Some of these judges were renowned heroes. Hebrews 11 names four of them in its "Hall of Faith" passage: Gideon, Barak, Samson, and Jephthah. Another notable judge is Deborah. The final leader in this succession of judges is Samuel (see 1 Samuel 7:15).

Although some great heroes and stories come out of the period of the judges, this was no way to live. It was not God's will that His people would be on a constant teeter-totter, vacillating between loyalty to God and apostasy. God wants unwavering devotion from His people, just as He remains faithful to us always. The cycle of disobedience and rescue could not continue indefinitely. Something needed to change.

Hannah

As Samuel's story begins, it is clear that societal change was sorely needed. His story also begins with the emotional account of a woman desperate for personal change. Her name was Hannah.

Hannah was married to a man named Elkanah. Elkanah also had another wife named Peninnah. The two women shared the same husband, but there was one major difference between them. Peninnah had children; Hannah did not.

---

5   Hummel, *The Word Becoming Flesh*, 114.

Elkanah tried to console Hannah by showing favoritism to her. When he went to offer a sacrifice, he gave one portion each to Peninnah and her sons, but "to Hannah he gave a double portion, because he loved her, though the LORD had closed her womb" (1 Samuel 1:5). However, he also proved to be somewhat dense when he asked why she was weeping one day and offered this misguided solace: "Am I not more to you than ten sons?" (v. 8).

Along with her own sadness, Hannah also had to endure the other wife taunting her! "Her rival used to provoke her grievously to irritate her" (v. 6).

Can you relate to Hannah? Maybe her struggle is yours. You and your spouse have desired a child, but so far, no pregnancy. Your friends are holding babies, talking about babies, attending baby showers, decorating nurseries. You see those round tummies and wonder, "Why her? Why not me?"

Or maybe you relate indirectly. The issue isn't a closed womb but a closed door.

You thought the interview went well, but you just got the phone call informing you that "you're an excellent candidate, but it wasn't the right fit." You got your hopes up—again—and the door was slammed in your face, again.

You've been estranged from a loved one for too long. You decided long ago that you're ready to make amends, but the other person refuses. Your calls go unreturned. Your emails go unanswered. You long to restore the relationship, but the door remains shut, locked from the other side.

Life's disappointments leave us feeling defeated. In these cases, we long for change. We crave it. And as people of faith, those desires become the focus of our prayers.

Prayer

Hannah's prayers were desperate pleas for changed circumstances. Scripture says, "She was deeply distressed and prayed to the LORD and wept bitterly" (1 Samuel 1:10). Deeply distressed. Wept bitterly. These words surround the statement that she prayed to the Lord. Her prayers were drenched in tears. Her prayers poured forth from a heart afflicted with sadness.

The passage continues:

> And she vowed a vow and said, "O LORD of hosts, if You will indeed look on the affliction of Your servant and remember me and not forget Your servant, but will give to Your servant a son, then I will give him to the LORD all the days of his life, and no razor shall touch his head." (v. 11)

Hannah promised that if God gave her a son, she'd give her son to God for a lifetime of service. Specifically, she pledged that her son would be a Nazirite, a special type of consecration to the Lord with stipulations detailed in the Mosaic Law (see Numbers 6).

Have you ever done that? Made a deal with God? "God, if You do this for me, I'll do that for You."

Hannah's prayer was answered as she desired. God granted her a son, Samuel. She interpreted Samuel's birth as an answer to her prayer. The name *Samuel* sounds like the Hebrew word meaning "heard of God."[6] She said in delight, "For this child I prayed, and the LORD has granted me my petition that I made to Him" (v. 27).

In addition to Samuel, God eventually blessed Hannah with five more children (see 2:21). What a remarkable reversal for a woman once burdened by barrenness!

---

6   See ESV Bible note on 1 Samuel 1:20.

Rather than say Hannah's story illustrates the power of prayer, we might say her example demonstrates the *mystery* of prayer. In Hannah's case, she prayed for a son, and God gave her a son. Her story mirrors stories like Sarah, Rebekah, Rachel, and Elizabeth. However, some women pray for a child but never have a child. Some people pray for healing but are not healed. Some pray for a job, admission to a school, or a financial turnaround, but those things don't happen. In some cases, the request and the result are a match. In other cases, the request and the result are exact opposites. Prayer is a mystery.

The mystery of prayer is an extension of the mystery of God. In our prayers, we're reaching out to God, whose ways are higher than our ways and whose thoughts are higher than our thoughts (see Isaiah 55:8–9). Prayer is more than bartering with God. Prayer is emptying ourselves before Him, holding nothing back.

> For a more in-depth exploration of the mystery of prayer, see chapter 14 in *Jesus Said What?* (CPH, 2023).

Hannah held nothing back. She expressed her distress. Her prayers were lifted up through tears of bitterness. God welcomes our prayers in whatever condition we find ourselves.

God Remembers You

At the end of the story, this is how the biblical author records God's response: "The LORD remembered her" (1 Samuel 1:19). The Bible teaches us repeatedly that God remembers us. "It is He who remembered us in our low estate, for His steadfast love endures forever" (Psalm 136:23).

When the Bible says God remembers us, it means more than "we're on His mind." It means He acts on our behalf. Take, for example, the exodus. After four hundred years of Egyptian enslavement, "their cry for rescue from slavery came up to God. And God heard their groaning, and God remembered His covenant with Abraham, with

Isaac, and with Jacob" (Exodus 2:23–24). God remembered His covenant. Did He forget it, and the people's cry suddenly refreshed His memory? No. In fidelity to His covenant, God was about to act on behalf of His people. He was about to prove Himself faithful to His promises. When God remembers, He acts.

What happened right after those words from Exodus? God called Moses through the burning bush to deliver His people.

This is God's track record. He hears the cries of His people and acts on their behalf—often through a deliverer. God heard the cries of Hebrew slaves and raised up Moses. God saw the plight of His people and raised up judges. God heard the desperate prayer of a solitary woman and granted her a son named Samuel.

Greatest of all, God heard the cries of all humanity and brought forth a Savior. In many ways, Samuel prefigures Jesus. Before there was a king, Samuel functioned in the threefold office of prophet, priest, and ruler. Jesus is the great Prophet—His words are the authoritative Word of the Lord. Jesus is the great High Priest—He intercedes for us with our heavenly Father and offered Himself as the sacrifice for our sins. And Jesus is the King of kings and Lord of lords, reigning over all things by His grace and power.

Hannah and Mary

If we see Samuel foreshadowing Jesus, we also see striking parallels between Hannah and Mary. In the biblical narrative, Hannah foreshadows our Lord's mother.

- Both women had "impossible" pregnancies. Hannah was infertile; Mary was a virgin.
- Each woman described herself as a "servant" of the Lord (1 Samuel 1:11; Luke 1:38).

- Each woman received a revelation about a child to be born. Eli told Hannah; the angel Gabriel told Mary.

- By God's grace, they each conceived a son who would be a mighty leader.

Each woman also sang a beautiful song of praise after her annunciation. Just as the women's stories have many similarities, their words of praise also have striking parallels.

Both songs begin with a personal declaration of God's greatness.

- Hannah's song: "My heart exults in the LORD" (1 Samuel 2:1).

- Mary's Magnificat: "My soul magnifies the Lord" (Luke 1:46).[7]

Both songs celebrate divine reversals—when God humbles the proud and exalts the lowly.

- Hannah: "The LORD makes poor and makes rich; He brings low and He exalts" (1 Samuel 2:7).

- Mary: "He has brought down the mighty from their thrones and exalted those of humble estate" (Luke 1:52).

Both songs describe God as providing for the hungry.

- Hannah: "Those who were hungry have ceased to hunger" (1 Samuel 2:5).

- Mary: "He has filled the hungry with good things" (Luke 1:53).

---

7   *Magnificat* is Latin for "magnify."

Both songs proclaim God as the protector of His people.

- Hannah: "He will guard the feet of His faithful ones" (1 Samuel 2:9).
- Mary: "And His mercy is for those who fear Him from generation to generation" (Luke 1:50).

Through Mary's Son, Jesus, we rejoice that the truths expressed in the songs of Hannah and Mary apply to us. The Lord fills us with His Word and Supper, and we pour forth thanksgiving in worship, exulting and magnifying the Lord. Through Jesus' death on the cross, the ultimate reversal has taken place: sinners like us, who are poor in spirit, are given the riches of God's eternal grace. Jesus satisfies the deepest hungers of our souls by being the bread of life and giving Himself to us through bread and wine. By God's mercy, we go forward in life, not in a spirit of fear but with confidence that almighty God protects and guides us.

By providing deliverers, including Samuel and ultimately Jesus, God has demonstrated His unfailing devotion to His people. If you, like Hannah, long for change, be assured: the Lord Almighty hears your prayers. He remembers you in your low estate. And He has power and grace to lift you up.

FOR DISCUSSION

1. "Something has to change." Tell about a time in your life when you thought these words.

2. If you could choose a positive change to happen in your life today, what would you choose?

3. Read Judges 21:25. What does it mean to do right in your own eyes? What effect does that have on a society? on a family?

4. Prayer is a mystery. What does Isaiah 55:8–9 teach us about the mystery of how God answers prayers?

5. When you pray, what do you hope to accomplish?

6. How do you tend to respond to God when it appears His answer to your prayer is "no" or "not right now"?

7. How do you see yourself in Hannah's story?

8. This chapter cites several similarities between Hannah and Mary. What personal qualities in these women do you admire?

9. Read Hannah's prayer in 1 Samuel 2:1–10. By reading her prayer, what do we learn about God?

CHAPTER 5

Personal Transformation

(1 SAMUEL 3)

And the LORD came and stood, calling as at other times, "Samuel! Samuel!" And Samuel said, "Speak, for Your servant hears."

1 SAMUEL 3:10

In 1957, John F. Kennedy was awarded the Pulitzer Prize for his book *Profiles in Courage,* a series of short biographies from eight American patriots. Kennedy knew about courage from personal experience.

Persevering through health struggles required courage. From childhood onward, Kennedy suffered from various ailments. He was hospitalized for months at a time and subjected to numerous painful examinations. He was near death more than once.

But his defining moment of courage occurred in World War II. He was commanding a torpedo boat in the middle of the Pacific Ocean. Out of nowhere, a Japanese submarine sliced the boat in half. Some men, including Kennedy, remained on the wreckage, while others were plunged into the water. One sailor, engineer Patrick McMahon, was splashing in the water, trying to stay afloat. Kennedy, who had been on the swim team at Harvard, jumped into the water. He bit down on one end of a belt while McMahon held on to the other end. Towing McMahon, Kennedy swam all the way to the nearest island. By the time they reached the island, Kennedy was so exhausted that McMahon had to pull him ashore. Six days later, after a series of events befitting an adventure novel, Kennedy and his surviving crewmates climbed aboard US rescue boats.

For his courage and leadership, Kennedy was awarded the Navy and Marine Corps Medal.[8]

A heroic rescue in the middle of the ocean demands courage. To some extent, adapting to change requires courage too.

When we face seismic shifts in our lives, it can feel like we've been tossed into a raging sea. Everything is turbulent. Nothing is calm. How do we navigate these times of transition? We need courage.

Eli the High Priest

The first major turning point in Samuel's life required courage. The stage is set in 1 Samuel 3:1: "Now the boy Samuel was ministering to the LORD in the presence of Eli. And the word of the LORD was rare in those days; there was no frequent vision."

Eli first appeared in 1 Samuel 1. When Hannah was at the temple praying for a son, Eli was there listening. Because her lips were moving but her prayer was unspoken, Eli mistakenly thought she was drunk. After she explained herself, Eli said to her, "Go in peace, and the God of Israel grant your petition that you have made to Him" (v. 17).

---

8   For more on this story, see "John F. Kennedy and PT 109," John F. Kennedy Presidential Library and Museum (website), www.jfklibrary.org/learn/about-jfk/jfk-in-history/john-f-kennedy-and-pt-109 (accessed September 16, 2022).

Coming from Eli, these words were a weighty pronouncement. The name *Eli* means "my God." Eli was the high priest of Shiloh, where the ark of the covenant resided. He was the second-to-last judge of Israel (Samuel was the last). He judged Israel for forty years (4:18). Eli had unparalleled spiritual clout, so his words to Hannah had significant gravitas.

Ironically, while Eli had great authority publicly, he failed to garner respect at home. Of his sons, Scripture says, "They would not listen to the voice of their father" (2:25). The Bible describes Eli's sons, Hophni and Phinehas, as "worthless men" (v. 12). Their sins included treating the offerings "with contempt" (v. 17) and sleeping with multiple women (v. 22). Because Eli's sons were unfit to succeed their father as spiritual leaders of Israel, God announced to Eli through an unnamed spokesman that his sons would be struck down. God declared, "I will raise up for Myself a faithful priest, who shall do according to what is in My heart and in My mind" (v. 35). Enter Samuel.

Samuel's Calling

The account recorded in 1 Samuel 3 is arguably the most well-known story about Samuel. It's the one that appears in children's Bibles and Sunday School lessons. A popular hymn, "Here I Am, Lord," recalls Samuel's words from this chapter.

Hannah promised to give her son to the Lord's service, and she fulfilled that promise. As the account begins, Samuel is sleeping in the tabernacle, a tent that housed the ark of the covenant. During the night, God called Samuel audibly. Samuel ran to Eli, assuming that Eli had summoned him. Eli said he never called Samuel and told the young man to go back to sleep. The events repeated: God again called; Samuel again ran to Eli; Eli again told him to return to bed.

When God called a third time, Samuel ran to Eli, but this time Eli realized it was God calling Samuel. Eli instructed Samuel to say,

"Speak, for Your servant hears" (v. 10). Samuel followed the script. And God gave Samuel his first assignment: a message for Eli.

That night, everything changed for Samuel. It all changed because God called him.

Did you know that God has called you? In Baptism, He calls you by the Gospel to "be His own and live under Him in His kingdom and serve Him in everlasting righteousness, innocence, and blessedness" (Small Catechism, Creed, Second Article). Through water and the Word, God places His promises on you.

Called by God, you're not the same anymore. You have a new purpose: to serve Him. You have new priorities: to share His love and spread the Gospel.

It works with us like it did with Samuel. We don't find God. He finds us. After the second time God called Samuel, Scripture says, "Samuel did not yet know the LORD, and the word of the LORD had not yet been revealed to him" (v. 7). God must reveal Himself to us. We know God because of His gracious self-revelation to us.

God chose Samuel, and by grace, He chooses us.

Office of Prophet

On that fateful night, the Lord called Samuel into the unique role of prophet. "And all Israel from Dan to Beersheba knew that Samuel was established as a prophet of the LORD" (1 Samuel 3:20). In the Bible, a prophet was someone who spoke for God. Sometimes prophets spoke about the future, but they were more than fortune-tellers. Prophets spoke the truth that God gave them to speak about the past, present, or future.

Before Samuel, only Moses fulfilled the role of prophet of Israel (Deuteronomy 34:10), though Abraham and Aaron were also labeled prophets (Genesis 20:7; Exodus 7:1). After Samuel, other prophets came along in the era of the kings. Some notable ones were Nathan, Elijah, and Elisha. At the end of 2 Kings, the first of the writing prophets to be mentioned by name is Isaiah (2 Kings 19:2). In the arrangement of the Old Testament books, Isaiah, Jeremiah, and Ezekiel are called the Major Prophets. The books of Hosea through Malachi are called the Minor Prophets, not because the messages are less significant but simply because the books are shorter than the Major Prophets. Daniel also was a prophet.

Three terms are attached to Samuel in establishing his identity:

Prophet. This term (or its plural) appears most often of the three in the Bible—470 times.[9] However, it's only used once to describe Samuel, in 1 Samuel 3:20. The Hebrew word is *nabi*, which means "spokesman" or "speaker."

Seer. This term (or its plural) appears 28 times in the Bible. With one exception, the word occurs exclusively in the books of Samuel, Kings, and Chronicles. Its first appearance indicates that it was an older term that fell out of use in spoken language by the time the books of Samuel were written. "Formerly in Israel, when a man went to inquire of God, he said, 'Come, let us go to the seer,' for today's 'prophet' was formerly called a seer" (1 Samuel 9:9). The word *seer* is applied to Samuel four times, all in 1 Samuel 9. The Hebrew word for seer is *roe*, a derivative of the common Hebrew word meaning "to see."

Man of God. This term appears 78 times in the Bible, all but two in the Old Testament. It was used most often when little information was known about a prophet. Perhaps his name was unknown or there was some mystery about his identity. This term is used four times to describe Samuel, also in 1 Samuel 9, when Saul is about to meet Samuel. The designation "man of God" also connects the prophets to Israel's first prophet, Moses (Deuteronomy 33:1).

All three terms describe Samuel. He spoke for God. He saw what God wanted him to see and communicated it to others. And he was very much a man of God—someone who lived his life for the Lord and walked with spiritual authority and authenticity.

---

9   These numbers are based on the ESV translation as counted on blueletterbible.org.

God's Definitive Spokesman

God selected Samuel as His spokesman, first to Eli and then to the entire nation. In Jesus, God's definitive spokesman arrived. Samuel and all the prophets foreshadowed the One who spoke with divine authority. Centuries before Samuel, Moses predicted such a leader: "The LORD your God will raise up for you a prophet like me from among you, from your brothers—it is to Him you shall listen" (Deuteronomy 18:15). Written centuries later, the New Testament book of Hebrews opens with these words: "Long ago, at many times and in many ways, God spoke to our fathers by the prophets, but in these last days He has spoken to us by His Son" (Hebrews 1:1–2).

Like Samuel, Jesus heard God's voice. Samuel was asleep when God spoke. Jesus was wide awake—He had just been baptized in the Jordan River! After the Holy Spirit descended as a dove and the heavens opened, the Father's voice thundered, "You are My beloved Son; with You I am well pleased" (Mark 1:11).

As God's Son, Jesus delivered divine truth to the world. Samuel's message came from God. In Jesus, God Himself spoke. No wonder the crowds "were astonished at His teaching, for He was teaching them as one who had authority" (Matthew 7:28–29). Jesus indeed had authority, surpassing the authority of the prophets.

Jesus declared His role as God's spokesman early in His public ministry when He spoke in His hometown synagogue in Nazareth. Quoting the prophet Isaiah, Jesus asserted,

> The Spirit of the Lord is upon Me, because He has anointed Me to proclaim good news to the poor. He has sent Me to proclaim liberty to the captives and recovering of sight to the blind, to set at liberty those who are oppressed, to proclaim the year of the Lord's favor. (Luke 4:18–19)

Notice that the word *proclaim* appears three times. Jesus understood His role as a proclaimer, a spokesman.

As 1 Samuel 3 wraps up, a marvelous statement appears: "And Samuel grew, and the LORD was with him and let none of his words fall to the ground" (v. 19). None of his words fell to the ground. They always hit the target: the human heart.

The same is true of Jesus' words. They didn't fall to the ground. They hit their target. Through His words, Jesus healed. Through His words, Jesus forgave sins. Through His words, Jesus raised the dead! His words inspired the masses, comforted the hurting, and communicated God's love to broken people. His words were, and are, power-packed: "The words that I have spoken to you are spirit and life" (John 6:63).

Even from the cross, His words hit their mark. Sweat and blood dripped from His body, saturating the dirt beneath His cross, but His words never fell to the ground. He interceded for His killers. He promised paradise. He entrusted His mother and the beloved disciple to each other. He quoted Scripture. He revealed the depths of His physical suffering. He declared the culmination of His work. He entrusted His spirit to the Father. These words live on forever, just as He, now risen, lives on forever.

The Word made flesh speaks a living word to us today. Through the words of the Bible, Jesus speaks to us. God's authoritative spokesman continues His ministry of delivering truth to us as we read His Word, hear it proclaimed, and trust in His life-giving promises.

Changing Roles

The role of spokesman was a significant one for Jesus, as it was for Samuel before Him. With his calling from God, Samuel found himself suddenly thrust into a new role and a new relationship with his mentor. God gave Samuel a message to declare to Eli . . . and it wasn't good news. The message was about Eli's sons, who were described as "worthless men . . . [who] treated the offering of the LORD with contempt" (1 Samuel 2:12, 17).

The bad news for Eli that God delivered to Samuel was this: "I am about to punish [Eli's] house forever, for the iniquity that he knew, because his sons were blaspheming God, and he did not restrain them" (3:13).

As you might imagine, Samuel was nervous about speaking such a dire message to his mentor. The Bible says that "Samuel was afraid to tell the vision to Eli" (v. 15). But Eli insisted on hearing the full report, so "Samuel told him everything and hid nothing from him" (v. 18).

God's first assignment for Samuel required courage! Change often does. Think about these facets of change that confronted Samuel:

Samuel needed courage to accept the reality of change. Once God called Samuel and made him a spokesman of divine truth, one chapter of Samuel's life was ending, and another was beginning.

Sometimes we struggle to accept that changes are real. We try to live in the past and pretend that things are the way they used to be, even though we know they're not. For parents, it can be hard to admit that their children are growing up and need more independence. For employees, it can be a struggle to accept someone has been promoted from peer to supervisor. For people who cherish a bygone era, it can be agonizing to watch society take an abrupt turn in a new direction. Sometimes we'd rather bury our heads and pretend that change isn't happening. We need courage like Samuel's to accept the reality of change.

Samuel needed courage to let go of his former identity. Samuel was still himself. But he was no longer Samuel the pupil. Called by God, Samuel could never revert to being an untested student under Eli. Those days had suddenly receded into the rearview mirror.

Sometimes our identity is tied to what used to be. When "what used to be" is no more, it can lead to feelings of grief and sadness. Endings can be extremely difficult. But letting go is an unavoidable component of change. Before we enter a new chapter, we have to close the old chapter. That takes God-given courage.

Samuel needed courage to embrace his new role. He was now a prophet. He was now a mouthpiece for the Lord. God designated Samuel before his birth, and the day had arrived for him to fully assume the part. After the ending comes the beginning.

Some roles may seem perfectly designed for us. I was speaking to a friend who began a new job a couple of years ago, and his workload and level of responsibility had increased dramatically. I asked how the job was going. He replied confidently, "It seems to be a fit." Other roles are a struggle to accept. Unemployed. Divorced. Widowed. Cancer patient. These roles are undesired. It can take a very long time to adapt to the demands of these challenging new roles. It takes God-given courage to embrace some new roles.

Samuel needed courage to interact according to his new relationship dynamics. He was accustomed to learning from Eli. Now Eli was going to learn from him. As the older man and the high priest, Eli had been Samuel's superior. But now, filled with God's word, Samuel was the authority, and Eli had to heed the younger man's words.

Role reversals can be uncomfortable. Adult children understand the tensions inherent in caring for aging parents. In some cases, an adult child must make decisions for a parent. A role reversal like that can be difficult to swallow, especially when the child asks for the car keys, access to bank records, or anything that feels like a loss of independence for the parent.

For these difficult, emotional changes, it's important to remember that if God is calling, the response of faith is "Here I am, Lord."

As Christians, God has called us to trust Him and love others. Sometimes love requires doing the hard thing when it's the right thing. For Samuel, it wasn't easy confronting Eli and announcing divine consequences. It wasn't easy for Samuel, but it was necessary because God called him to do it.

God calls you into your vocations. Husbands and wives, God placed you into a covenant relationship with each other. He called you to love and sacrifice for each other, "submitting to one another out of reverence for Christ" (Ephesians 5:21). Children, God placed you in a family. He called you to "honor your father and mother" (6:2). Moms and dads, God called you to a holy responsibility—to bring up your children "in the discipline and instruction of the Lord" (v. 4). Workers, God placed you in a job so that you could contribute to society and provide for others. He has called you to do your best, "rendering service with a good will as to the Lord and not to man" (v. 7). It takes God-given courage to interact according to new relationship dynamics.

Courage and Change

The concluding sentences of 1 Samuel 3 remind us to be courageous and entrust the results to the Lord. We can understand Samuel's nervousness over speaking God's word of Law to Eli. Certain scenarios could have been playing in Samuel's mind. *What if Eli gets angry with me? What if he kicks me out and I have to live on the street? What if he, the high priest, counters with a word of judgment on me? What if I heard God wrong, and I create a stir for no good reason?*

Whatever worst-case scenario Samuel may have envisioned, Eli's reaction showed the effectiveness of God's Law. Eli replied, "It is the LORD. Let Him do what seems good to Him" (1 Samuel 3:18). To Samuel's relief, Eli responded graciously. He could have reacted harshly, but he didn't. Clearly, the Lord was in the midst of their conversation.

Navigating change requires courage. And God gives us courage, as we're strengthened through Word and Sacrament, filled with grace and power through faith in Christ. As God once spoke to Joshua, He now says to us: "Have I not commanded you? Be strong and courageous. Do not be frightened, and do not be dismayed, for the LORD your God is with you wherever you go" (Joshua 1:9).

Even when the waters of change are turbulent, we can go forward and trust in the Lord. He is with us! We have the Savior's promise: "I am with you always" (Matthew 28:20). He rescued us from the wreckage of our own sin. He is the One who pulled us safely to shore in the safe embrace of His loving arms.

We go forward courageously. The Lord is with us!

FOR DISCUSSION

1. Samuel apprenticed under Eli. Have you ever learned a trade under someone or studied under someone's tutelage? What were the joys and challenges of learning under a mentor?

2. God has called you in Baptism. How is your calling in Baptism similar to Samuel's calling in the night? How is it different?

3. Which words of Jesus have hit the mark in your heart? If you need an example of Jesus' words to consider, read Matthew 6:25–34.

4. This chapter lists four facets of change that Samuel confronted (see pp. 68–69). Which of the four have you dealt with recently?

5. On page 70, the author shares Bible verses with instructions about honoring God in various vocations. Choose one vocation in your life and share how God may be calling you to step up your game in that role.

6. Do you ever think of worst-case scenarios? What is the harm in thinking of these scenarios? Is there any benefit to envisioning negative scenarios?

7. Samuel had an intimidating task: to relay the Lord's stern message to Eli. Think of a time you had to be the bearer of difficult news. How did you feel going

into the conversation? How did the conversation turn out?

8. God spoke to Samuel audibly in the night, a unique experience. Still today, people sometimes speak about actually hearing the voice of God speaking to them. Is that possible? What cautions might be appropriate if someone claims to hear God talking to them?

9. Jesus promises us, "I am with you always" (Matthew 28:20). How might these words help you live more courageously?

CHAPTER 6

Having the Right Mindset

(1 SAMUEL 7)

Samuel judged Israel all the days of his life. And he went on a circuit year by year to Bethel, Gilgal, and Mizpah. And he judged Israel in all these places. Then he would return to Ramah, for his home was there, and there also he judged Israel. And he built there an altar to the Lord.

1 SAMUEL 7:15–17

Having the right mindset is crucial for navigating our changing world.

Many professional athletes understand the importance of getting into the right mindset. They're intentional about how they spend their time leading up to a game.

Some athletes calm their nerves by thinking about things other than the upcoming competition.[10] Olympic sprinter Usain Bolt liked to occupy his mind with conversations about topics unrelated to running. Some of his favorite topics included fast cars and music. Olympic rower Nareg Guregian distracted himself by scrolling through social media for thirty minutes and then listening to music on the way to competitions. Former Major League Baseball pitcher A. J. Griffin relaxed before games by strumming on his guitar. His teammates listened as he played Led Zeppelin and Spanish standards.

Then there's former National Football League running back Curtis Martin. Before plowing his way past a bunch of three-hundred-pound linemen, Martin spent valuable pregame minutes reading his Bible! His favorite pregame passage was Psalm 91, which assures safety under the protection of God, our refuge and fortress.

Before facing a challenge, I can't think of a better way to get into the right mindset than by reading God's Word. We're doing that in our study of Samuel's life and ministry!

A Challenging World

Our changing world poses a big challenge to us as Christians. Studies show that, statistically, Americans are turning away from Christianity. According to the Pew Research Center, as recently as the 1990s, about 90 percent of American adults identified as Christians. Today, far fewer, about two-thirds of adults, make that same claim.[11]

---

10 The following pregame rituals are described in Sarah Sommer, "10 Habits of Highly Successful Athletes," *Men's Journal* (website), December 4, 2017, www.mens journal.com/adventure/10-habits-of-highly-successful-athletes-20131203/ (accessed September 1, 2023), and Lily Ford, "What to Steal from 6 Olympians' Pre-Game Rituals," *Men's Journal* (website), December 4, 2017, www.mensjournal .com/sports/what-to-steal-from-6-olympians-pre-game-rituals-w434233/ (accessed September 1, 2023).

11 "Modeling the Future of Religion in America," Pew Research Center (website), September 13, 2022, www.pewresearch.org/religion/2022/09/13/modeling-the -future-of-religion-in-america/ (accessed September 1, 2023).

The current trend suggests a continued decline in the number of people who believe in Christ, know the teachings of Scripture, and seek to live out those teachings.

In analyzing the societal drift away from Christian teachings and values, authors Ben Freudenburg and Rick Lawrence compellingly argue that out of the Ten Commandments, our culture regards only the Seventh Commandment as binding—stealing can still land an offender in jail. In their book *The Family-Friendly Church,* the authors contend that the other Commandments are no longer a part of our society's moral compass. Consider these examples:

- False religions and cults continue to attract followers, directing seekers away from the one true God (First Commandment).
- People flippantly misuse God's name in daily conversation (Second Commandment).
- Authority figures, such as teachers, are regularly disrespected (Fourth Commandment).
- Many politicians have turned giving false testimony into an art form (Eighth Commandment).
- Our consumer culture is built on coveting (Ninth and Tenth Commandments).[12]

It's an alarming trend! As we engage with a society that is increasingly secular and sometimes hostile toward Christianity, what should our mindset be? By carefully observing Samuel's leadership in a changing culture, we find indispensable guidance.

---

12   See Ben Freudenburg and Rick Lawrence, *The Family-Friendly Church* (Loveland, CO: Group Publishing, 1998), 11.

Samuel Speaks Out

Samuel's society was shifting in many ways, some of them terribly distressing.

For a period covering more than twenty years, Scripture reports nothing about Samuel. God called Samuel in 1 Samuel 3, but he vanishes from the narrative in chapters 4 through 6. These chapters describe a tragic fiasco—the capture of the ark of the covenant—and a remarkable reversal, the return of the ark, after a series of afflictions forced the Philistines to cry uncle! As chapter 7 opens and Samuel reenters the narrative, we see a culture in shambles.

Idolatry! That's a cultural shift Samuel never desired. But he wasn't given a vote. It was a cultural movement that swept in through generations of unfaithfulness by God's chosen people.

Sadly, spiritual drift was nothing new. The Bible records other acts of disloyalty to God. At Mount Sinai, to Moses' dismay, the people worshiped a golden calf. Years later, Moses' successor, Joshua, told the people to "put away the foreign gods that are among you, and incline your heart to the LORD, the God of Israel" (Joshua 24:23). After Samuel, David was loyal to God, but his son Solomon accommodated the religious practices of his foreign wives, including their false gods.

God forbids any form of idolatry in the First Commandment: "You shall have no other gods before Me" (Exodus 20:3). The Lord is a jealous God who requires complete loyalty. "I am the LORD; that is My name; My glory I give to no other, nor My praise to carved idols" (Isaiah 42:8). In the New Testament, Paul wrote, "You cannot drink the cup of the Lord and the cup of demons" (1 Corinthians 10:21). It's one or the other—the true God or false gods. To drift away from God is to drift away from what is good, right, and true.

To combat the cultural drift of Samuel's day, the Lord raised up Samuel and gave him the unique platform of judge. As discussed previously, a judge was divinely empowered to rescue God's people from an oppressor. In this case, idols had captured the hearts of God's people, and it was time to liberate them.

So, emboldened by the Holy Spirit, Samuel gathered all of Israel to a place called Mizpah and addressed them. Samuel's words are instructive for having the right mindset toward our changing world. The prophet is quoted three times in 1 Samuel 7. Each statement contains valuable wisdom for us.

Clashes with Culture

Samuel's first words in chapter 7 remind us:

Christianity and culture are bound to clash.

Our world is broken by sin. The enemy, Satan, exacerbates the brokenness in every way he can. Don't expect the ways of the world to align with the ways of faith. Expect challenges. Anticipate incompatibility between what the Bible teaches and what the world touts.

Samuel confronted the brokenness of his society with his words at Mizpah. "If you are returning to the LORD with all your heart, then put away the foreign gods and the Ashtaroth from among you and direct your heart to the LORD and serve Him only, and He will deliver you out of the hands of the Philistines" (1 Samuel 7:3).

These words of Law convicted Samuel's hearers, as their actions demonstrated: "So the people of Israel put away the Baals and the Ashtaroth, and they served the LORD only" (v. 4). Baal and Ashtaroth were foreign gods represented by statues that the Israelites sinfully incorporated into their own religious practices. Because Samuel boldly used his platform, these menaces to the Israelite religion were discarded, and the people returned to the Lord.

Jesus, too, instructed people to forsake false gods, targeting the counterfeit deities of His day. In the Sermon on the Mount, Jesus told people to put away these false gods:

- *Lust (the god of sexual desire).* "I say to you that everyone who looks at a woman with lustful intent has already committed adultery with her in his heart" (Matthew 5:28).

- *Boastfulness (the god of other people's opinions).* "Beware of practicing your righteousness before other people in order to be seen by them, for then you will have no reward from your Father who is in heaven" (Matthew 6:1).

- *Materialism (the god of possessions).* "Do not lay up for yourselves treasures on earth. . . . You cannot serve God and money" (Matthew 6:19, 24).

- *Worry (the god of control).* "Do not be anxious about your life, what you will eat or what you will drink, nor about your body, what you will put on" (Matthew 6:25).

- *Hypocritical judgment (the god of superiority).* "Why do you see the speck that is in your brother's eye, but do not notice the log that is in your own eye?" (Matthew 7:3).

To broken people wrapped up in sin, Jesus said, "Repent, for the kingdom of God is at hand" (Matthew 4:17). Jesus speaks those words to us today, commanding us to put away the false gods of our culture and to return in faith to the one true God, who sent His Son to rescue us from our sins.

People of Prayer

Samuel's second statement in 1 Samuel 7 reminds us:

We are to be people of prayer.

After the people put away the false gods and returned to the Lord, Samuel instructed, "Gather all Israel to Mizpah, and I will pray to the LORD for you" (1 Samuel 7:5).

Through the inspired Word of God, we see unmistakable evidence of the power of prayer. Abraham pleaded for God to refrain from destroying people who had incurred His wrath, and God relented (Genesis 18:16–33). Moses entreated God to preserve His chosen people, even after they sinned greatly, and God honored Moses' humble request (Exodus 33:12–23).

Jesus taught about prayer through a parable of a persistent widow. With relentless tenacity, she pestered a judge for a favorable ruling until she got it. Luke writes that Jesus told the "parable to the effect that they ought always to pray and not lose heart" (Luke 18:1).

When we pray, we come before the almighty Maker of the universe, asking for His intervention and gracious actions. That's what Samuel did. In their distress, the people said to him, "Do not cease to cry out to the LORD our God for us" (1 Samuel 7:8). The Bible tells us, "And Samuel cried out to the LORD for Israel, and the LORD answered him" (v. 9).

You and I are given the platform of prayer through Jesus. He is the great High Priest who grants us access to the Most High. The writer to the Hebrews encouraged, "Let us then with confidence draw near to the throne of grace, that we may receive mercy and find grace to help in time of need" (Hebrews 4:16). Our Lord's throne is one of grace. He awaits our prayers. He is our constant source of help—our refuge and strength in time of need (see Psalm 46:1)!

Our capabilities have a limit. Some things only God can do. You and I can't redirect the tides of cultural change, but we can commend our concerns to the Lord. In faith, we entrust all our cares to Him with confidence that He hears us and answers according to His perfect will.

Never underestimate the power of prayer! Our changing world challenges us in many ways. Some things are beyond our control. But nothing is beyond God's control! When we feel powerless, remember who has the power. God does, and our prayers to Him make a difference.

God's Record of Faithfulness

Samuel's third statement in 1 Samuel 7 teaches us:

God's record of faithfulness gives us confidence in the face of uncertainty.

As promised, Samuel prayed for the people. As he presented a burnt offering to the Lord, the Philistines approached to attack. Then—BOOM!—with a thunderous sound, God threw the Philistine soldiers into confusion. The Israelites pursued them and overwhelmed the enemy. To commemorate the victory, Samuel set up a stone called Ebenezer, a combination of two Hebrew words meaning "help" and "stone." He said, "Till now the Lord has helped us" (1 Samuel 7:12). Samuel was reminding the people of God's faithfulness in the past to encourage them about the future.

Undesired changes can unnerve us and cause us to worry about what other adversities are on the horizon. Worries about the future can drain us of joy in the present moment.

Whenever we're frazzled about the future, we can shift our mindset to one of remembrance and faith. We don't know how the future will shape up. But God's past actions are already accomplished. Nothing changes what God has already done. What has He brought you through? What obstacles have you overcome by His strength? How has He lifted you up when you were downcast? We each have a testimony of God's faithfulness to us. He is our Ebenezer, our rock of help.

Most important, we can look to Jesus' work on the cross as God's definitive act of faithfulness. Despite our sin, God remained faithful; He didn't abandon His creation. He sent us a Savior who was crucified and then laid behind a stone. This stone was not a rock of help but an obstacle—a seal to His tomb. Pontius Pilate ordered the tomb to be sealed with a stone and posted a guard so that no one would steal Jesus' body and claim that He had risen, as He predicted (see Matthew 27:66).

But then on the third day—BOOM! An earthquake shook the ground and an angel descended from heaven, rolled back the stone, and sat on it. The angel announced to the women that Jesus had risen! Through personal appearances, Jesus confirmed the angel's message.

Jesus' resurrection, a past event, gives us hope for the future. Our future is secured—eternally—because of the Savior who lived, died, and rose for us! With confidence, we carry that message of hope into a world desperately in need of truth and grace.

A Voice for Good

The church, the people of God, carry forth Christ's message of repentance, inviting all to turn from sin and turn to God. We are in the world but not of the world. We are to be salt and light, standing out from the crowd. Through His Word, God clarifies our stance: "Do not be conformed to this world, but be transformed by the renewal of your mind, that by testing you may discern what is the will of God, what is good and acceptable and perfect" (Romans 12:2). Conformity? No. Transformation through faith in Christ? Yes!

As transformed people, we seek to bring transformation to the world around us in whatever ways the Lord enables us. You have a voice. You can use your influence in a positive way.

You—yes, *you*—have influence.

You might feel like your platform is insignificant. Don't believe that. Platforms come in all shapes and sizes. Samuel's story reveals that.

In Samuel's first words in 1 Samuel 7, he addressed "all the house of Israel" (1 Samuel 7:3). As the chapter closes, we read that he also engaged smaller audiences. The closing verses say that "Samuel judged Israel all the days of his life. And he went on a circuit year by year to Bethel, Gilgal, and Mizpah. And he judged Israel in all these places. Then he would return to Ramah, for his home was there, and there also he judged Israel. And he built there an altar to the LORD" (vv. 15–17).

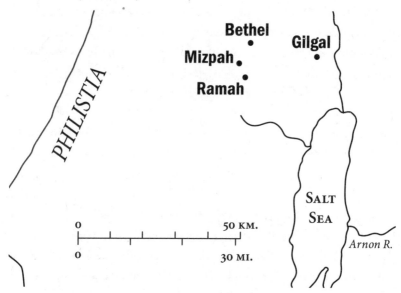

We don't know the size of gatherings in Bethel, Gilgal, Mizpah, and Ramah. Maybe crowds flocked to Samuel like he was a rock star, or maybe his audiences were merely a handful of interested listeners. Either way, it's clear that Samuel regularly spoke to audiences smaller than "all the house of Israel."

Some people speak in front of thousands. Others have only a few contacts. But with those individuals, they have influence, so those contacts matter greatly.

For many, your most significant audience is your family. Parents, please take this to heart: you have unparalleled influence on your children. You and I may not be able to redirect the cultural flow, but we can shape the worldview of the children God entrusts to us.

More than anyone else, parents shape their children's beliefs and convictions. A couple of years ago, I began to evaluate how I'm shaping my children's values and behaviors. I decided to take my two oldest boys on a father-child retreat so we could have time together in a relaxed setting. It was wonderful. We talked on the two-hour drive. At camp, we learned together, played together, explored together, and bonded. We returned to camp the next year with my daughter for an equally meaningful weekend. Like all Christian parents, my wife and I have the unique opportunity to shape disciples for the Lord, trusting in the promise of God's Word: "Train up a child in the way he should go; even when he is old he will not depart from it" (Proverbs 22:6).

In His Word, God tells parents to make the most of their platform as family leaders. Speaking of God's Commandments, Moses said, "You shall teach them diligently to your children, and shall talk of them when you sit in your house, and when you walk by the way, and when you lie down, and when you rise" (Deuteronomy 6:7). Day after day, parents can reinforce God's truths to impressionable young minds. In the formative years of our children's upbringing, we have a platform and a God-given responsibility to train them up in the Lord.

Family leadership also includes grandparents, aunts, uncles, and others who are respected for their experience and wisdom. Even those who are young in years can be messengers of God's timeless truth, just as Samuel was a messenger of truth as a young man.

A church functions similarly. Along with pastors, other leaders include elders, board members, staff, and key volunteers. Within the family of faith, respected leaders have a valuable platform for speaking truth to those under their spiritual care.

Whatever your station in life, your thoughts and words matter. They matter as you stand on the solid foundation of God's Word, regardless of which direction the winds of cultural change blow. As God's people, we're not merely passive observers of a constantly changing world. We're active participants, bringing a message of hope that transforms lives and eternities.

FOR DISCUSSION

1. If you were raised as a Christian, what did your parents do to cultivate faith in you?

2. Why do you think more and more Americans are drifting away from Christianity?

3. This chapter discusses the idea that the only commandment our society honors is the Seventh Commandment, "You shall not steal." Do you agree or disagree with this cultural analysis? Explain your answer.

4. Describe the spiritual state of God's people before Samuel gathered them at Mizpah.

5. This chapter includes examples of false gods that Jesus preached against. Which of these false gods do you feel has the greatest pull on people's hearts today? Or can you think of one not on the list?

6. What does it mean to "speak the truth in love" (Ephesians 4:15)? What effect does it have on people when you speak the truth in love?

7. Who influences you most directly? How do you strive to have a positive impact on their lives?

8. You have a platform for spreading the message of God's grace in Christ. Describe a time you shared your faith with someone.

CHAPTER 7

Handling Disappointing Developments

(1 SAMUEL 8)

And the LORD said to Samuel, "Obey the voice
of the people in all that they say to you, for
they have not rejected you, but they have rejected
Me from being king over them."

1 SAMUEL 8:7

Occasionally a destitute man or woman will wander into the church building and ask for a pastor. It's obvious at first glance that the person is worn down and overburdened. Often the individual is seeking financial assistance. Usually they have a story to share.

"I do yard work, but with the drought, no one's grass is growing. My income is practically nothing right now."

"I just moved here for a job, but the company had to cut workers, and I was one of them. I don't have any family or friends in town. I need help paying for a motel room until I figure out where I'm going to live."

"Cancer treatments have drained my savings. I need help paying my electric bill."

No one sets out to be broke. No one's vision of life includes having to ask for money or moving to a new town and being jobless or spending all your savings on medical treatments. These people became needy because of disappointing developments in their lives.

Disappointments

When events unfold in an unexpected and undesired way, we're left staring at the gap between how we envisioned life going and how it actually turned out. Your disappointing developments may not have drained your bank account or emptied your pockets, but they may have drained hope from your heart or emptied your spirit of its vitality. Poverty of spirit is a legitimate hardship too.

In my survey of church members and colleagues, when asked about personal changes that have been difficult to accept, many people cited times when life went very differently than they expected.

Divorce was on the list. No one stands at the altar and commits to marriage expecting the marriage to fall apart. For that matter, no dad gives his daughter away anticipating that the marriage will be short-lived. The pain of divorce ripples through a family, affecting everyone involved.

Family life includes other hardships. Young couples often are asked, "How many kids do you want to have?" But family size isn't always within our control. One respondent cited "infertility" as a disappointing development. Another wrote, "Not having as many children as I thought I would."

For parents, watching children wander from their faith is agonizing. One respondent wrote that a difficult personal development was their "kids drifting from the church/God."

Issues with aging can be disappointing developments. A respondent wrote that the hardest changes to accept have been "physical and mental deterioration—lost dreams because of the needs of daily circumstances." Some people retire with visions of traveling and playing with grandchildren. Instead, as health issues arise, their calendars are booked with one doctor appointment after another.

Career disappointments can be difficult to accept. One person wrote about struggling with "the changes in my career and what I thought would happen to me." Another wrote about "whenever God says 'no' to my plans, like for careers that I thought He was leading me toward."

Life doesn't always go the way we planned.

A Prophet Rejected

Samuel's life also contained disappointing developments. A growing dissatisfaction among the Israelites swelled into a demand for change at the top—the very top!

The demand began with a sharp complaint: "Behold, you are old and your sons do not walk in your ways. Now appoint for us a king to judge us like all the nations" (1 Samuel 8:5).

The complaint contains two themes of personal disappointments.

First, Samuel was old. Aging brings with it disappointments. As we age, we slow down. Along with that, people may make assumptions about our capabilities as we get older.

Second, the people deemed Samuel's sons unfit to lead. That part of the complaint must have really stung. Aging is expected. But children walking in disobedience to the Lord—that was a surprising development. The people's accusation was accurate. First Samuel

8 includes these words: "Yet his sons did not walk in his ways but turned aside after gain. They took bribes and perverted justice" (v. 3).

PKs (pastor's kids) have a lot of pressure to follow in Dad's footsteps as a spiritual leader. Many do. Some take a different path. In Samuel's case, surprisingly, he fared no better than Eli as a dad. Eli was godly, but his sons weren't. Samuel's face could have adorned a Mount Rushmore of spiritual leaders, but his sons were greedy and unjust. Surely Eli and Samuel felt the pain of parents saddened that their children had wandered from the Lord. Sometimes spiritual drift happens in spite of parents' best intentions and efforts.

Did Samuel kick himself? Did his self-talk go something like this? *How could this happen to me too? I promised myself I'd learn from what happened with Eli and his sons. I didn't want my sons to turn out this way!* We don't know Samuel's exact thoughts. No doubt, he was disappointed.

With those dual complaints—Samuel's age and his unjust sons—the Israelites issued their demand: "Appoint for us a king to judge us like all the nations" (v. 5). They rejected the leadership of Samuel's family line and insisted on a change in government.

God Understands Disappointment

The demand for a king was not only a rejection of Samuel and his sons. Chiefly, it was a rejection of God and the unique covenant relationship He had established with His people.

During Moses' time, God made provisions for a king to eventually lead His people (see Deuteronomy 17:14–20). The demand for a king didn't surprise God. It didn't catch Him off guard. It didn't throw off His plans. He had anticipated it. He always sees what's around the corner, and He always has an answer for every dilemma that sinful humanity generates.

The people insisted on a king "to judge us like all the nations." This expectation defied God's intent for His people. He promised in the days of Moses: "You shall be My treasured possession among all peoples, for all the earth is Mine; and you shall be to Me a kingdom of priests and a holy nation" (Exodus 19:5–6). God wanted a one-of-a-kind, exclusive relationship with Israel, but Israel wanted to be like every other nation.

Likewise, the church of Christ receives from God a unique status as "a chosen race, a royal priesthood, a holy nation, a people of His own possession" (1 Peter 2:9). We're not meant to be like everyone else. We're meant to be different. God has called us out of darkness so that we shine as lights in the world. The church is set apart to provide a contrast to the ways of the world. Rather than follow the crowd, as God's people, we are to embrace our unique calling.

The Perfectly Obedient Son

As God's people, we don't always live up to the holy calling He has placed on us. We don't always walk in His ways.

Samuel's sons did not follow in his spiritual footsteps. Consequently, we might understand how the people felt justified in rejecting them.

But by that measurement, how do we explain the rejection of Jesus? He walked flawlessly in His Father's footsteps. Jesus said, "Truly, truly, I say to you, the Son can do nothing of His own accord, but only what He sees the Father doing. For whatever the Father does, that the Son does likewise" (John 5:19).

Nonetheless, the people rejected God's perfectly righteous Son. "He came to His own, and His own people did not receive Him" (John 1:11). What a huge disappointment! Beginning in the Garden of Eden, after the fall into sin, God laid the groundwork: He promised to provide a Savior. God reaffirmed that promise through numerous prophecies. He even sent an immediate forerunner, John the Baptist, to prepare the way of the Lord. But when Jesus came to the very people who had heard the promises and yearned for the Messiah, they rejected Him.

In Jesus, they had a king—the King of kings and Lord of lords. In a statement dripping with irony, Pontius Pilate presented Jesus to a crowd and declared, "Behold your King!" (John 19:14). If only Pilate knew Jesus' true identity! If only the people knew! But the people shouted, "Crucify Him!" (v. 6). To prevent trouble from Rome, they declared, "We have no king but Caesar" (John 19:15).

The egregious error from Samuel's day repeated itself in Jesus' day—Israel rejected God as its king.

Return of the King

For Jesus' disciples, His death was a disheartening disappointment. They left everything to follow Him. They listened to His authoritative teachings. They witnessed His incredible miracles. It was unthinkable that someone so powerful would die, seemingly before His time had arrived. When Jesus predicted His death, His disciples protested. Peter declared, "Far be it from You, Lord! This shall never happen to You" (Matthew 16:22).

The disappointments continued. On Sunday morning, the women saw the tomb was empty. Mary Magdalene ran and told Peter and John. They examined the tomb and confirmed that it was indeed empty. They had not only a dead Master, they now had a missing Master.

But their disappointment turned into joy. As Mary Magdalene stood weeping outside the tomb, she looked inside and saw two angels who spoke to her. Then she turned and saw a man she was unable to recognize through her tears. He spoke to her, and she realized who it was! Jesus! Alive again!

From that point forward, Jesus would never be missing again. Before ascending to heaven, He promised His disciples, "Behold, I am with you always, to the end of the age" (Matthew 28:20). Christ is risen, and He is present with His people.

In 2022, Queen Elizabeth II of the United Kingdom died after seven decades on the throne. After her death, all eyes turned to her successor. Since she was the longest reigning monarch in British history, her son Charles had the longest wait of any heir to the throne. How would he conduct himself as King Charles III?

In one of his first public appearances, King Charles emerged from a car amid a throng of well-wishers who lined the street. He then walked over to the people and began to shake hands. For minutes that must have seemed like hours to his security detail, King Charles interacted with his subjects—hand to hand, flesh to flesh.

Our Lord Jesus is not a distant king, insulated from His subjects in a castle far away. Jesus, who once came near in His incarnation, abides with His people. He draws near through His Word, through the waters of Baptism, and through the royal banquet of Holy Communion. A king can't come closer than giving you His very body and blood!

Though the world rejects Him still today, Jesus is King and governs all things in heaven and on earth as a benevolent, loving ruler.

Reframing the Problem

Scripture tells us that the people's demand "displeased Samuel" (1 Samuel 8:6a). What did he do with those feelings? "Samuel prayed to the LORD" (v. 6b). The prophet poured himself out to God, aware of God's great compassion.

God invites us to do the same when we face disappointing developments. When the Bible says to "pray without ceasing" (1 Thessalonians 5:17), that includes moments of heartache when life doesn't go the way we thought it would. We direct our prayers to God, who says, "Call upon Me in the day of trouble; I will deliver you, and you shall glorify Me" (Psalm 50:15).

We find comfort in God. The hymn "What a Friend We Have in Jesus" says it beautifully: "Oh, what peace we often forfeit; Oh, what needless pain we bear—All because we do not carry Ev'rything to

God in prayer!" (*LSB* 770:1). God has a limitless supply of peace to share with us when we cast our cares on Him.

As Samuel poured out his disappointment in prayer, the Lord responded with words of assurance. God reminded Samuel that he, Samuel, wasn't the ultimate leader. God was. Therefore, the people weren't rejecting Samuel. They were rejecting God's leadership through the prophet.

The Lord said, "Obey the voice of the people in all that they say to you, for they have not rejected you, but they have rejected Me from being king over them" (1 Samuel 8:7).

We tend to take things personally. Our egos get bruised easily. When things don't go our way, we get bent out of shape, assuming we're the problem, that it's a reflection on us, that we've failed.

Notice that God didn't point the finger at Samuel. God didn't condemn Samuel for his sons' waywardness or the people's rebellion. God absorbed the hit Himself. He said the people were rejecting Him. In love, God gave Samuel a new perspective for seeing his problem. *God reframed the issue so that Samuel could go forward with clarity and peace.*

God continued by telling Samuel to give the people a fair warning: life would not be all roses under a human king. Like other human kings, theirs would be a sinner who would rule with a heavy hand. A human king would force their sons into military service. A human king would task their daughters with making perfumes and food. A human king would confiscate the best of their lands and a portion of their harvests. A human king would treat his subjects as slaves.

Still interested in a human king?

"Yes!" the people insisted.

So be it.

When the dust settled and it was clear that a human king was forthcoming, Samuel had a major change to process in his heart. He had to come to terms with a disappointing development.

Tips for Navigating Disappointment

Have you found yourself in the same boat—having to come to terms with a disappointing development? Just as God reframed Samuel's problem to give clarity and peace, God's Word can reframe our thinking to lead us forward in faith. Here are some principles for handling disappointing developments:

Permit yourself to feel disappointed. God gave us feelings. Change is often about loss, and losses need to be grieved. Remember the words about change from Ecclesiastes 3? There is "a time to weep, and a time to laugh; a time to mourn, and a time to dance" (Ecclesiastes 3:4). We do ourselves no favors when we repress our emotions, pretending we're okay when we're really not. We grieve disappointments with faith, trusting Jesus' promise: "Blessed are those who mourn, for they shall be comforted" (Matthew 5:4).

Focus on what you can control. In the middle of Romans 12:18 is an easily overlooked but crucial phrase: "If possible, *so far as it depends on you,* live at peace with all" (italics mine). You can't control some things. They don't depend on you. You can't control the weather or gas prices or the stock market or traffic on the highway. You can't control other people's actions or decisions, including decisions that affect you. You can only control your attitude and your reaction.

Process with someone else. God designed us for community. Scripture instructs us, "Bear one another's burdens, and so fulfill the law of Christ" (Galatians 6:2). Whom can you turn to? Perhaps it's a friend, a parent, a sibling, or a mentor. Sometimes we're shy about telling others our problems because we don't want to be a burden. Or we're embarrassed or afraid that others will think less of us. In fact, most of the time, people are honored that you'd entrust them with your burdens, and they want to help, even if that help is simply listening.

Choose a positive mindset. Paul wrote, "Let all bitterness and wrath and anger and clamor and slander be put away from you, along with all malice" (Ephesians 4:31). It's natural to feel emotions deeply, but it's not healthy for disappointment to morph into bitterness or for anger to harden our hearts. Choosing a positive mindset is not the same as denying pain and pretending all is bliss. Choosing a positive mindset is refusing to be stuck in misery.

Seek to learn. In Proverbs 4:5, God's Word instructs us, "Get wisdom; get insight." Much wisdom comes through life experience . . . processed thoughtfully. We can learn a lot about life and about ourselves through disappointments. Ask yourself: How can I grow through this experience? What can I learn? How can I become a more resilient person? This type of reflection can turn hardship into a golden opportunity for personal growth.

Keep your hopes fixed heavenward. Disappointments are harsh reminders that we live in a fallen world, and to some extent, we'll never be fully satisfied in this life. We're wired to yearn for a greater existence, transcending earthly woes. The Bible says, "He has put eternity into man's heart" (Ecclesiastes 3:11). With eternity in mind, Paul wrote, "For this light momentary affliction is preparing us for an eternal weight of glory beyond all comparison, as we look not to the things that are seen but to the things that are unseen" (2 Corinthians 4:17–18).

Remember God's faithfulness. Through it all, we can trust in God and His plan. Scripture declares, "Know therefore that the LORD your God is God, the faithful God who keeps covenant and steadfast love with those who love Him and keep His commandments, to a thousand generations" (Deuteronomy 7:9). Covered by the blood of Christ, you are incorporated into His covenant people. Throughout the highest mountains and lowest valleys of life, His steadfast love endures for you.

Holding on to Jesus by faith, you can survive and grow through disappointing developments. The King has you firmly in His hands.

FOR DISCUSSION

1. Tell about a time—good or bad—when life went differently than you expected.

2. Read 1 Samuel 8:5. What thoughts do you think went through Samuel's mind when the people voiced their complaint?

3. Why did God say that the people were rejecting Him and not Samuel?

4. Through Samuel, God warned Israel about the drawbacks of a human king. Aware of the negatives, why did they persist in demanding a human king?

5. Why did God allow Israel to have a human king?

6. The last section of this chapter contains principles for dealing with disappointing developments. One is to process with someone else. Who typically fills that role for you? How has that person helped you work through feelings of disappointment?

7. Another principle is to choose a positive mindset. How easy or hard is it for you to choose a positive mindset?

8. Still another principle is seeking to learn. What have you learned from disappointments?

9. The final principle listed is to remember God's faithfulness. What does it mean to remember God's faithfulness? How does such remembrance provide strength in the midst of disappointing developments?

Adapting to a New Person

(1 SAMUEL 9:1–10:16)

Samuel answered Saul, "I am the seer. Go up before me to the high place, for today you shall eat with me, and in the morning I will let you go and will tell you all that is on your mind."

1 SAMUEL 9:19

Following in the footsteps of an established leader can be challenging. My predecessor, Pastor Dan Mueller, pastored Shepherd of the Hills Lutheran Church in San Antonio for thirty-six years. I arrived fresh out of the seminary as he was entering his thirtieth year of ministry at the church. He was an institution; I was a rookie.

Thankfully, Pastor Dan was committed to my success as he prepared me, and the congregation, for his impending retirement. We divided preaching duties evenly so people could become accustomed to a new voice. Even though he had long-term relationships with almost every member, he allowed me to make many of the hospital visits. We shared Baptisms, funerals, and weddings. He always affirmed me publicly. In those ways, Pastor Dan positioned me for success, and for that, I'm grateful.

Being the new guy isn't easy. You may know that from firsthand experience.

Maybe you're the new person at work. You're trying to fit in, but since the rest of the team has a long history together, you feel like an outsider.

Or maybe you're the new leader. The previous boss had a distinct leadership style, and yours is different. It's a learning curve for you and everyone else. If you were promoted from within, you face a unique challenge. Your coworkers knew you as a peer. Now you're in charge. When you walk into the room, conversation halts. (The good news: they feel obligated to laugh at your jokes now!)

Joining a family can be a major adjustment. Just ask a young man who has married into a family whose dynamics are night-and-day different from his family of origin—it's like being on a different planet! Or ask the stepmother who's seeking the respect of children whom she didn't birth but is now rearing as her own.

When you're the new person, change takes on a face. *You* are the change.

Saul

Change was coming for Israel, and it had a name: Saul.

What does the Bible record about Saul?

When we meet him in 1 Samuel 9:2, he's a handsome young man . . . and tall. He was a head taller than everyone else—the starting center for the Holy Land High School basketball team!

Saul was from the tribe of Benjamin, descended from Jacob's youngest of twelve sons. Apparently Saul came from an upper-class family. His father, Kish, was "a man of wealth" (v. 1).

His kingship started out well. Anointed by Samuel. Proclaimed king by the people. Victorious in early military conflicts.

Then things fell apart, as upcoming chapters will demonstrate. In his impatience, Saul went out of his lane, subverting the Lord's prophet. Then Saul disobeyed explicit directions from God. For these sins, Saul forfeited his royal line. As Saul's future successor, David, gained stature, Saul burned with jealousy and became violent. Insecure and desperate to know his future, Saul consulted a witch, an ungodly act. Finally, Saul and his son Jonathan died in battle—mortally wounded, Saul fell on his own sword.

Those events come later in 1 Samuel. For now, we encounter a young man fresh on the scene. In Saul's first biblical appearance, his father's donkeys were lost. Unable to locate the donkeys, Saul was ready to return home. His servant suggested that they consult a "man of God" who resided nearby (1 Samuel 9:6). That man was Samuel.

Thanks to a divine heads-up, Samuel was expecting him.

Samuel's Humility

Put yourself in Samuel's sandals. As mentioned, Samuel was a rare leader who occupied all three offices of prophet, priest, and leader. He spoke for God, he offered sacrifices, and he was the government and military leader. When Saul became king, Samuel had to relinquish one of his offices. He had to share power.

Samuel could have resisted. He could have balked at God's instructions to anoint Saul. But defying God never turns out well. Another selfish tactic could have been to anoint Saul but then undermine him—bad-mouth him behind his back, get in his way, interfere with his initiatives. By obstructing the new king, maybe the people would long for the good old days when Samuel did everything.

Sometimes we're needy about being needed. When a new person arrives, we can feel threatened. We can become resentful and wish that the intruder had never invaded our turf.

As a man of God, Samuel didn't take that approach. Instead, he humbled himself and served Saul. He did his best to position the new king for success. When they met, Samuel outlined his plan. "Samuel answered Saul, 'I am the seer. Go up before me to the high place, for today you shall eat with me, and in the morning I will let you go and will tell you all that is on your mind'" (1 Samuel 9:19).

Samuel committed to serve Saul in two ways: through a meal and through words.

At a dinner party for thirty, Samuel seated Saul at the head of the table. This was no Happy Meal or TV dinner. The meal was a generous supper, including a savory portion of leg meat normally reserved for the priest (1 Samuel 9:24; see Leviticus 7:32–33).

Samuel also provided a rooftop bed for Saul to spend the night. The flat rooftops of homes were frequently used as places of sleep and conversation. In the Middle Eastern heat, the open air of the rooftop was a great place to catch a cool breeze.

The next day, they journeyed onward. Samuel instructed Saul to send his servant ahead so that it would be just the two of them—the outgoing judge and the incoming king. Samuel told Saul he was ready to "make known to you the word of God" (1 Samuel 9:27).

Then Samuel kissed Saul and poured oil on his head, anointing him as king.

Samuel immediately became the king's minister of information. He informed Saul about the people he would meet, an offering of bread he would receive, and a special gifting of the Holy Spirit that would rush upon him (10:6).

And as icing on the cake, Saul learned the donkeys had been found (see v. 16)!

Anointed One

By pouring oil on Saul, Samuel formally designated Saul for a special office: "to be prince over His people Israel" (1 Samuel 10:1). Anointing has a long and rich history in the Bible. It always indicates someone or something being set aside for God's unique purpose. Anointing was a Spirit-filled ritual for new beginnings.

At Mount Sinai, as the priestly garments were being designed, God specified that Aaron and his sons "shall be anointed in them and ordained in them" (Exodus 29:29).

With Saul, anointing became associated not just with priests but also with the king. David, Solomon, and future kings also were anointed as they were installed into their royal office. The Psalms pray for God to protect His anointed one, referring to the Davidic king.

Isaiah pointed ahead to a coming King with these words: "The Spirit of the Lord GOD is upon me, because the LORD has anointed me to bring good news to the poor" (Isaiah 61:1). While preaching at the synagogue in Nazareth, Jesus applied these words to Himself. He was almost stoned to death for calling Himself the Lord's anointed (see Luke 4:18).

The Hebrew word for anointed is *masiah*—from which we get the word *Messiah*. When Jesus arrived, the people had been waiting centuries for a Messiah, a leader anointed by God to deliver His people.

Some recognized Jesus as a man sent from God. One woman was so overwhelmed to be in His presence that she stood behind Him, weeping. She wet His feet with her tears and wiped them with her hair. Then, Luke tells us, she "kissed His feet and anointed them with the ointment" (Luke 7:38). The woman did her own anointing of God's chosen one, giving Him honor and love from a humble heart.

Christ's Humility

Soon, however, Jesus was the one humbling Himself on the cross. Jesus was anointed by God for a specific purpose: to save the world from sin. To do that, He became a sacrifice, willingly suffering in our place.

Jesus' descent actually began before the cross. It began the moment Jesus assumed human flesh, as the Apostles' Creed teaches. Consider these statements from the Creed:

Conceived by the Holy Spirit. By His incarnation, Jesus lowered Himself from heaven to earth. The infinite became bound by the laws of nature. He confined Himself to a human body. He was subject to gravity. He was prone to injury and illness. In His humanity, Jesus emptied Himself of His heavenly prerogatives and became a servant.

Born of the Virgin Mary. Christ was born in poverty. His parents were working class. He was born in a second-rate location "because there was no place for them in the inn" (Luke 2:7). His mother laid Him in a manger, a feeding trough for animals. His first visitors were lowly, dirty shepherds.

Suffered under Pontius Pilate. Months of heated opposition culminated in His suffering. The religious leaders felt threatened by Jesus' popularity. They paid Judas to betray Jesus. Another kiss was given to God's anointed, this time not in honor or devotion but in disloyalty. Following Judas's cue, soldiers arrested the innocent Son of God and marched Him away. Jesus endured false accusations and unjust trials. He humbly submitted Himself to the governing authorities, including Pontius Pilate, who sentenced Jesus to death.

Was crucified. The cross was the ultimate humiliation. Jesus endured indescribable physical suffering. Bystanders hurled insults at Him. He was made a spectacle, displayed publicly for all to see. Raised up on a cross, He was brought low in shame and contempt

CHAPTER 8 · ADAPTING TO A NEW PERSON (1 SAMUEL 9:1–10:16)

as He suffered the ultimate pain—the pain of separation from His Father as He was punished for our sins.

Died. The Lord of life breathed His last.

And was buried. As one last indignity, He was laid in a borrowed tomb.

Jesus humbled Himself, but His story didn't end there. In a timeless moment, His downward trajectory suddenly reversed. After proclaiming victory to the spirits in hell (see 1 Peter 3:19), He rose from the dead. He ascended into heaven and reclaimed His rightful seat at the Father's right hand. Now we await the return of the true King to judge the living and the dead.

Humble Means

As surely as Christ lives, He comes to His people to position us for success in fulfilling His mission.

During His earthly ministry, Jesus predicted His departure. His earthly ministry would end, but His mission would endure. For that reason, He trained apostles (literally, "sent ones") to carry on His work. He promised the Holy Spirit. And He delivered on that promise, pouring out the Holy Spirit on Pentecost and providing that same Spirit to all believers to comfort, strengthen, and empower His people for ministry.

To bring His Spirit into our lives, Jesus comes to us through humble means. As Samuel served Saul through a meal and words, Jesus does the same for us.

Christ's meal is not just nutrition for our bodies. His meal is nourishment for our souls. Through ordinary bread and wine, Christ communes with us in His body and blood. He strengthens us for the journey of life.

Christ's words are not just information for our minds. His words are promises to uplift us and propel us forward in this life and into eternal life. "Truly, truly, I say to you, whoever hears My word and believes Him who sent Me has eternal life" (John 5:24).

When we encounter Jesus through Word and Sacrament, we move in an upward trajectory. Bolstered by His promises, we're lifted out of the slimy pit of our sin and seated "in the heavenly places in Christ Jesus" (Ephesians 2:6). Filled with His grace, we redirect our focus away from this worrisome world and instead set our minds "on things that are above, not on things that are on earth" (Colossians 3:2).

Supporting Newcomers

With our minds fixed on Christ and things above, we don't need to feel threatened about anyone or anything in this world. Our status as God's children is secure. In Christ, our purpose is firm as His ambassadors in this world. With that assurance, we can humble ourselves and serve those who may need a boost as they get started in a new role.

When a new person walks in the door, it can be a major change for everyone involved. If a new person has stepped into your life, you can apply some key lessons from Samuel about humility and service.

Be available. Learning the ropes can be a challenge. Many times, a new person becomes discouraged and is tempted to give up. Samuel made himself available to Saul. The prophet committed significant time, energy, and resources to help Saul feel comfortable and supported in his new role. From the outset, Saul knew that Samuel was there for him.

Attend to the newcomer's overall well-being. Extend an invitation to dinner at your house. Ask how the person's family is doing. Encourage rest and rejuvenation after times of intense work. Samuel welcomed Saul, fed him, and had a bed prepared for him. The prophet made sure that Saul's physical needs were met, ensuring that the king-designate was nourished and rested for the pivotal events in front of him.

Spend time one on one with the newcomer. Giving your time shows that you care. Samuel gave individual attention to Saul. The prophet told Saul to excuse his servant so that Samuel could have a one-on-one conversation with him. Private conversations are good settings for speaking candidly and being vulnerable. A new person may have frustrations to share or questions that aren't suitable for an audience.

Share information generously. If you have longevity, you probably possess valuable institutional knowledge. More background information can help a new person navigate unfamiliar waters. Samuel made known to Saul "the word of God" (1 Samuel 9:27), including information Saul needed going forward.

Be willing to let go. You can't give away responsibility while holding onto it at the same time. Many new people have been undermined because their predecessors insisted on retaining functions that needed to be fully released. When Samuel anointed Saul "to be prince over His people Israel," Samuel relinquished a portion of leadership. Samuel stepped back so Saul could step up.

Through Samuel, we learn about welcoming newcomers and positioning them for success. As God's children, our status before the Lord is secure. Rather than operating out of insecurity, we can serve others from a reservoir of confidence based on who we are in Jesus. May God grant each of us a Christlike spirit of humility so that we, too, can support others in their new beginnings!

FOR DISCUSSION

1. Tell about your experience as the new person. What was it like at first? Did anyone help you get acclimated? How did you adapt?

2. Why do you think God chose Saul as the first king if Saul would eventually mess it up?

3. What did Samuel do to support Saul?

4. How difficult do you think it was for Samuel to give up a portion of his leadership? What do you think helped him overcome his misgivings and do the right thing?

5. Share about a time you had to step back so someone else could step up.

6. Why do you think Saul was anointed privately instead of publicly? What were the advantages of a private anointing?

7. God was calling both Samuel and Saul into new roles. How can you tell if God is calling you to something new?

8. The end of the chapter gave several suggestions on how to support a newcomer. What from the list stood out to you? What would you add to the list or delete from it?

CHAPTER 9

Being an Advocate for Others

(1 SAMUEL 10:17-27)

And Samuel said to all the people, "Do you see him whom the LORD has chosen? There is none like him among all the people." And all the people shouted, "Long live the king!"

1 SAMUEL 10:24

Picture the scene in modern-day terms: A spotlight is shining on a lectern bearing the royal insignia. News cameras are rolling. The nation waits eagerly. There's a buzz in the crowd. Anticipation is at a fevered pitch.

An announcer booms over the loudspeakers, "Introducing . . . the king!" And onto the stage steps . . . no one.

Where was the first king of Israel?

Saul was hiding.

Who could blame him after Samuel's introduction?

To publicly present Israel's first king for the first time, Samuel once again gathered the people at Mizpah, the same place where he interceded for them in 1 Samuel 7. This time, the prophet began by reviewing God's credentials: rescue from Egyptian slavery and from oppression by other kingdoms. Then Samuel delivered a punch to the gut, telling the people, "But today you have rejected your God, who saves you from all your calamities and your distresses, and you have said to Him, 'Set a king over us'" (1 Samuel 10:19).

Quite a setup for Saul, wouldn't you say? Here's Samuel saying, in essence, "You stubborn people don't appreciate all that God has done for you! Let me now present to you the man who will occupy the kingly office that your rebellion has made necessary!" What an introduction! Who would want to be a living monument of the people's rejection of God?

Was Samuel positioning Saul for success or failure?

Where Is the King?

Lest the people think that Samuel single-handedly picked the king, the prophet made it clear that God did the choosing. He brought all the tribes together, and "the tribe of Benjamin was taken by lot" (1 Samuel 10:20). We're not exactly sure what the process of taking by lot involved. According to *The Lutheran Study Bible*, it was a "method to determine God's will," and "the process required faith that God would indeed guide the choice, as well as a willingness to abide by the choice as being from God" (*TLSB* note on Joshua 4:2). The process of lots then narrowed to the Benjaminite clan of the Matrites, and from within the clan of Matrites, "Saul the son of Kish was taken by lot" (1 Samuel 8:21).

There it was! By a mysterious divine selection process, Saul had been chosen as the king.

The only problem was . . . Saul was nowhere to be found! He was hiding!

After catechism class at my church, if we have extra time, we have a tradition of playing hide-and-seek indoors. Certain areas are off-limits. But of the areas that are fair game, it's amusing to observe the clever hiding spots that students devise. It's always a fun surprise to open the clothing donation box and see a seventh grader crammed inside with his legs folded up like a pretzel!

Sometimes the students choose such good hiding spots that I have to recruit the already-found students to help locate the missing ones.

The people couldn't find Saul anywhere. So they had to seek help. Whom did they ask? God, the all-seeing one!

"And the LORD said, 'Behold, he has hidden himself among the baggage'" (v. 22).

The people rushed to the baggage, pulled Saul out, and brought the new king into public view. Saul tried to hide, but there was no hiding from God's call.

Despite the people's sinful intent in demanding a human king and despite Saul's hesitancy to be king, Saul was God's chosen one.

Being God's Chosen One

One of the most daunting challenges is to be God's chosen person in circumstances you'd never choose. That's the challenge Jesus faced. No one would choose the cross. Yet Jesus submitted Himself to death to forgive our sins. Even when adversaries tempted Him, Jesus held firm to His purpose. Luke's Gospel says that as bystanders watched Jesus dying, "the rulers scoffed at Him, saying, 'He saved others; let Him save Himself, if He is the Christ of God, His Chosen One!'" (Luke 23:35).

From sinful lips unwittingly came the Gospel truth: Jesus was the Chosen One. Even in a wrong situation—the picture of injustice—Jesus was committed to being the right person and doing the right thing. He stayed on the cross until He breathed His last and finished His saving work.

Jesus fulfilled His role as God's anointed, and by faith in Him, we become God's chosen ones! God's Word declares of all believers, "But you are a chosen race, a royal priesthood, a holy nation, a people for His own possession, that you may proclaim the excellencies of Him who called you out of darkness into His marvelous light" (1 Peter 2:9).

Even in situations you would never choose, God has designated you to shine His light in the darkness. Scripture says, "Put on then, as God's chosen ones, holy and beloved, compassionate hearts, kindness, humility, meekness, and patience, bearing with one another" (Colossians 3:12–13). Even when subjected to undesired circumstances, we live out our calling as God's children, His chosen ones.

Support and Opposition

Our text from 1 Samuel 10 features a pair of chosen ones. Saul is the first chosen one. Samuel announced it to all the people: "Do you see him whom the LORD has chosen? There is none like him among all the people" (1 Samuel 10:24). As a young king, Saul did well. But over time, he ceased to be the right person. To summarize, his sad story includes disobeying God in critical moments, forfeiting his royal line, attempting to murder his own son Jonathan and the next king David, desperately consulting a witch, and tragically taking his own life. Saul was God's chosen one but fell short of his calling.

The other chosen one here is Samuel. God called Samuel as a boy and guided him through a lifetime of service. Whereas Saul was disappointing, Samuel rose to the occasion. Even in an unwanted circumstance—appointing a human king—Samuel obeyed the Lord. Samuel grieved the nation's rebellion, but he adhered to God's instructions and announced to the people, "Do you see him whom the LORD has chosen?" Samuel threw his full prophetic authority behind Saul. Samuel put aside his wounded feelings, instituted the monarchy, and supported the new leader.

Saul would need this support. The new king needed the backing of the revered prophet.

At the end of the chapter, Samuel sent everyone home. Saul, too, returned to his home. That's when the grumbling began. "But some worthless fellows said, 'How can this man save us?' And they despised him and brought him no present" (1 Samuel 10:27). It didn't take long for the critics to arise and begin planting seeds of dissension. They refused to honor the new king with their words or actions. No respect. No gift. No support.

Why the mixed reaction to Saul? The Bible doesn't tell us, but we can infer possible reasons.

Perhaps the opposition resented that Saul was from the tribe of Benjamin. Benjamin, descended from the youngest of Jacob's twelve sons, was the smallest tribe. Benjamin also was the tribe that fought against the other eleven in the period of the judges. A long-standing family feud among the tribes could have been a reason for the complaints against Saul as king.

Saul also didn't make a stellar first impression. By appearances, he looked like an imposing leader since he was a head taller than everyone else. Based on his initial actions, however, he didn't present himself well. Hiding among the baggage isn't the best way to inspire confidence from your subjects. Remember, the people of Israel demanded a king to lead them into battle and subdue other nations. They wanted a leader who was bold, aggressive, zealous. They wanted a lion, not a scaredy-cat!

To his credit, Saul responded to the negativity admirably. The Bible simply says, "But he held his peace" (1 Samuel 10:27). If the opposition did get under his skin, he wasn't going to give them the satisfaction of knowing it. He was the king, whether they agreed with the selection or not. He kept his cool and moved forward.

Change: A Lightning Rod for Criticism

Saul represented a major change. And major changes have a way of attracting critics.

"I don't like these new policies."

"Why can't we go back to the way we used to do things?"

"I told them this new way isn't going to work! But did they listen to me? No! We'll see how long it takes before they give up."

To build on a concept from the last chapter, sometimes the change isn't a policy or a program. Sometimes it's a person.

Saul symbolized change. People directed their criticism at him. People will do that to one another.

Family members may shake their heads about a new in-law: "I told her not to marry him."

Employees may gripe about a new supervisor: "I really didn't think she deserved the promotion."

Parishioners may lament about a new pastor: "His sermons just don't speak to me like our former pastor's. And I had to introduce myself three times before he remembered my name!"

Often, our shortcomings are easy to spot, and it doesn't take long for the critics to pounce. What a blessing to have someone who is willing to stand by you and advocate for you, in spite of your imperfections!

In many cases, when the family patriarch says, "Welcome to the family! I'm so glad you're one of us," the rest of the family takes its cue and becomes more receptive to the new in-law.

Many times, when an influential coworker says, "Hey, give her a chance to do her job before you judge her," the rest of the team becomes willing to cooperate with the new boss.

Likewise, when the longtime member and Sunday School teacher says how much he appreciates the depth and thoughtfulness of the new pastor's sermons, others tend to see his strengths in a way they hadn't considered before.

When you're the change, having a powerful ally can make all the difference.

Our Advocate

We have the most powerful ally of all: our Savior, Jesus.

In His earthly ministry, Jesus often spoke up for others. One example took place right before Holy Week. Jesus and His disciples visited Bethany and attended a dinner party hosted by His dear friends Martha, Mary, and Lazarus, whom Jesus had restored to life! Mary took a pound of expensive perfume and poured it on Jesus' feet to anoint Him. The house was filled with the fragrance, but one of the disciples was filled with hostility. Judas, Jesus' eventual betrayer, criticized Mary's extravagance, asking, "Why was this ointment not sold for three hundred denarii and given to the poor?" (John 12:5).

Jesus stepped quickly into the role of advocate and told the erring disciple to back off. "Leave her alone, so that she may keep it for the day of My burial. For the poor you will always have with you, but you do not always have Me" (vv. 7–8). Our Lord was not shy about standing up for someone who had done no wrong.

Even for someone who had done wrong, Jesus was willing to speak up. A few chapters earlier in John's Gospel, a woman was caught in adultery. As her accusers prepared to stone her—and presumptuously asked for Jesus to endorse her punishment—Jesus surprised them with a comment that went right to the heart: "Let him who is without sin among you be the first to throw a stone at her" (John 8:7). One by one, the woman's accusers departed, and she stood alone with Jesus, her advocate.

As Jesus stood up for others in His earthly ministry, He also is our defender, who stood up for us on the cross. Jesus humbled Himself to be spat upon, struck, flogged, and shamefully mistreated to be the

Advocate before the Father for all of us. He allowed Himself to be punished, not out of weakness or timidity, but out of strength—the strength to restrain Himself from making a defense.

In submitting Himself to death, Jesus fulfilled the words of Isaiah the prophet: "He was oppressed, and He was afflicted, yet He opened not His mouth; like a lamb that is led to the slaughter, and like a sheep that before its shearers is silent, so He opened not His mouth" (Isaiah 53:7). While on trial, Jesus didn't make a case for His innocence. He went to the cross for *our* guilt. By His willing sacrifice, we are set free from sin and eternal punishment.

Our Advocate in Heaven

Today Jesus continues His work of divine advocacy.

As our risen and ascended Lord, Jesus sits at the Father's right hand interceding for us (see Romans 8:34). The great Easter hymn "I Know That My Redeemer Lives" beautifully connects Jesus' resurrection with His ongoing intercession for us in heaven: "He lives to bless me with His love; He lives to plead for me above" (*LSB* 461:3).

His heavenly intercession is a key component of our salvation, as the Bible teaches in Hebrews 7:25: "Consequently, He is able to save to the uttermost those who draw near to God through Him, since He always lives to make intercession for them." This verse comes in the middle of a section in Hebrews that speaks of Jesus as our great High Priest. Of Jesus' threefold office—Prophet, Priest, and King—His work as our mediator with the Father is His priestly function. A priest goes between God and man. In the Old Testament, the priest offered sacrifices and prayers to God on behalf of the people, and the priest spoke truth and blessing from God to the people. The Old Testament priest was an image of the great High Priest who would die, rise, and intercede for us.

In Jesus, you never have to worry about your standing before God. Christ's intercession is constant. The verse from Hebrews says that our Lord Jesus "always lives to make intercession for them." He always lives—He is risen forevermore!—and therefore He is always making intercession for us. Because of that, our relationship with the Father is secure eternally.

Being an Advocate

In times of change, a strong advocate can make all the difference. Might you be that advocate for someone else?

Just as Samuel backed Saul, you also have opportunities to speak up on behalf of others. Whether it's a new family member, a new boss, or a new pastor, you can speak on behalf of people who represent change.

"If he loves her enough to marry her, we can learn to love her too."

"Give him a chance. He'll do a good job if we give him a fair chance."

"This is the man God called to serve us. We need to support him."

You may be God's chosen instrument to bring health into an environment of change. A gracious advocate can do that. A gracious advocate comes alongside someone and provides the support that's needed to go forward.

I knew a man in Houston who ran ultramarathons. A marathon is 26.2 miles. An ultramarathon is any distance beyond 26.2 miles. This man, Mark, ran an ultramarathon that was—ready for this?—100 miles!

At mile 80, as you might imagine, his legs were beyond tired. They were rubber, and he still had 20 miles ahead of him. Then, out of the stands, a tall figure darted onto the course. Mark's friend Kevin began to run alongside him. Kevin had never run a marathon. But to support his friend Mark, Kevin had secretly trained to run 20 miles so he could run alongside Mark and encourage him to finish the race. And he did. They did—together.

We all need someone to run alongside us, especially in times of adjustment and transition. You can be that person for someone else. It might require some extra effort, some sweat and toil, some uneasiness. But if you're willing, you can do a lot of good by being an advocate, a faithful ally.

Jesus, our heavenly ally, empowers us to graciously accept and defend others in this way.

FOR DISCUSSION

1. Why do you think Saul hid when he was announced as king? Do you see his actions as a positive sign of humility or a negative sign of weak leadership?

2. Why do you think Samuel went through the process of casting lots when he already knew that God had selected Saul as king?

3. Shortly after Saul's coronation, the people grumbled against him. What does grumbling reveal about human nature?

4. The Bible says that Saul "held his peace" in response to the negative reception. What does that response say about Saul?

5. Major changes have a way of attracting critics. Why might this be?

6. Read John 7:53–8:11. We don't know what happened to the woman. How do you think this encounter with Jesus as her advocate changed her?

7. When has someone advocated for you? How did it make you feel?

8. When have you advocated for someone else? What effect did your support have?

CHAPTER 10

Anchored in Faith

(1 SAMUEL 12)

> Moreover, as for me, far be it from me
> that I should sin against the LORD by ceasing
> to pray for you, and I will instruct you in
> the good and the right way.

1 SAMUEL 12:23

The other day, a church member approached me and said, "Pastor, I need you to give me an encouraging word." She felt overwhelmed and overburdened. She needed to hear something uplifting.

Perhaps you can relate. Times of change can cause stress. When life is moving faster than you can keep up, when the world you once knew has vanished, when the familiar is a distant memory, when you've suffered one loss after another, you can become discouraged and feel defeated. You may crave words of encouragement, something to lift your spirit. Similarly, in their distress, others may look to *you* for reassurance.

When someone is counting on you to speak uplifting words, where do you start? Samuel shows us. Toward the end of his leadership tenure, when he was "old and gray" (1 Samuel 12:2), Samuel delivered a farewell speech. The monarchy was in place, and the prophet was transitioning out.

Saying Farewell

Before encouraging his listeners with Gospel words, Samuel first confronted them with the Law.

To begin the speech, Samuel established his credibility as an honest leader with a legacy of faithful service. Samuel then reviewed God's history of faithfulness to His people, going back to Jacob, Moses, and the judges.

After that, Samuel's tone was stern. This was not a feel-good speech! He reminded the crowd of their wickedness in rejecting God and demanding a human king. He punctuated his speech by calling on the Lord to send thunder and lightning.

You may remember that thunder from the Lord has a way of disrupting a group. In 1 Samuel 7, as Samuel was sacrificing a burnt offering, the Philistines tried to attack. With a loud thunder, God threw the Philistines into complete disarray, and the Israelites routed the enemy.

In 1 Samuel 12, God once again sent thunder, this time not to disorient but to reorient. As intended, nature's fireworks got the people's attention, and the people responded in distress. They pleaded, "Pray for your servants to the LORD your God, that we may not die, for we have added to all our sins this evil, to ask for ourselves a king" (1 Samuel 12:19). Fearing death at that moment may seem overly dramatic. But the Bible teaches that "the wages of sin is death" (Romans 6:23). Death comes to all of us eventually because we're all sinners. Because of their rebellion, the people feared that their lives were in jeopardy.

To people in distress, Samuel spoke words of wisdom and reassurance. He pointed his listeners to God and anchored them in faith in the midst of anxiety. His approach provides a helpful framework for us in speaking to the distressed.

Samuel's Words

First, Samuel acknowledged the problem. He began, "Do not be afraid; you have done all this evil" (1 Samuel 12:20a). He acknowledged the reality they were facing.

He didn't overemphasize the problem. He wasn't rubbing their faces in it. He didn't dwell on it.

He also didn't dismiss or minimize the problem. He didn't rationalize it or justify it.

He named the reality. He acknowledged it. They had erred royally by rejecting God and insisting on human rule. They had invited trouble with their ungrateful demands. Thankfully, the mess was not beyond redemption.

Second, Samuel announced a path forward. He instructed, "Yet do not turn aside from following the LORD, but serve the LORD with all your heart" (v. 20b). Right after acknowledging their problem, he announced a path forward. The path forward was to follow God and serve Him wholeheartedly. The past was done. It was time to establish a new and better future.

Third, Samuel affirmed God's faithfulness. The prophet assured, "For the LORD will not forsake His people, for His great name's sake, because it has pleased the LORD to make you a people for Himself" (v. 22). God honors His promises. The people of Israel were heirs of God's covenant with Abraham: "I will establish My covenant between Me and you and your offspring after you throughout their generations for an everlasting covenant, to be God to you and to your offspring after you" (Genesis 17:7). Though Samuel's audience had rejected God, God remained committed to them.

Fourth, Samuel assured them of his prayers. Samuel felt strongly about prayer! "Moreover, as for me, far be it from me that I should sin against the LORD by ceasing to pray for you" (1 Samuel 12:23). Samuel was displeased with the people's disregard for God. However, he continued to love and pray for them. He called it a sin not to pray for them! Have you ever thought of prayer that way? You have the power of prayer at your disposal. By God's power, your prayers are able to help others. It would be a sin to let that power lie dormant!

Jesus' Words

We see a similar formula in Jesus' ministry—a ministry of acknowledging the problem, announcing a path forward, affirming God's faithfulness, and assuring intercessory support.

Jesus acknowledged the problem. Our greatest problem is our sin. Right off the bat in His ministry, Jesus addressed humanity's chief dilemma, saying, "Repent, for the kingdom of heaven is at hand" (Matthew 4:17). These words inaugurated Jesus' public ministry. When He was ready to begin preaching and teaching, His opening word was "Repent!"

What comes to mind when you hear the word *repent*? Perhaps you picture a confrontational message—a street preacher waving a sign or a highway billboard declaring, "Repent or perish." Perhaps *repent* evokes feelings of guilt—"You should be sorry" or "You should feel bad about your mistakes." Maybe you hear it as a call to action—a call to straighten up and get your act together. For some people, the word *repent* carries baggage and is a downer of a word. *Repent*, however, is Jesus' word to us. It is a word of divine invitation to turn from sin and turn to God for forgiveness and a new start.

Jesus told His listeners to repent because of an event: the arrival of God's kingdom. When Jesus entered this world, He brought the kingdom of heaven with Him. Wherever the king is, there is the kingdom. Jesus is the King of kings and Lord of lords. The reign of heaven accompanies Him wherever He goes.

Jesus announced a path forward. The path is Jesus Himself! He said, "I am the way, and the truth, and the life" (John 14:6). For sinners like you and me who get lost in a forest of confusion and wander from God's good path, Jesus is the way! For vulnerable people like us who believe the lies that assault us from an ungodly culture, Jesus is the truth! For mortals like us, subject to decline and decay, Jesus is life!

Jesus is the path forward. He not only acknowledges the problem of sin, He also bore our sin on the cross. Through the cross, He forgives our sin. From the cross, grace flows. His first words on the cross were "Father, forgive them, for they know not what they do" (Luke 23:34). Forgiveness is His gift to us. By trusting in Christ's finished work on the cross, we embrace His solution to our problem, the only thing that can cleanse us from sin: the blood of the Lamb.

Jesus affirmed God's faithfulness. Because of Jesus' death for us and His resurrection, we have peace in knowing that God is by our side in all things. God has promised never to forsake His children. Jesus experienced the pain of separation from our heavenly Father so that we never will. On the cross, Jesus cried out, "My God, My God, why have You forsaken Me?" (Matthew 27:46). By dying for our sins, Jesus restored us to God and made us heirs of the promise: "I will never leave you nor forsake you" (Hebrews 13:5).

Jesus assured His followers of prayer. Jesus promised, "So everyone who acknowledges Me before men, I also will acknowledge before My Father who is in heaven" (Matthew 10:32). In the last chapter, we learned about Jesus as our intercessor. What comfort we have in knowing that Jesus advocates for us at the highest level, the very throne of God!

Our Words

You and I will encounter people in distress—many of them struggling because of changes in their lives. When you encounter someone in distress, someone who needs encouragement, remember the formula:

- Acknowledge the problem.
- Announce that there is a path forward.
- Affirm God's faithfulness.
- Assure the person of your prayers.

"I'm so sorry you're going through this. I can see why you're feeling upset." Words like those acknowledge the problem and validate the person who is struggling. A while back, I read about a man's experience with well-meaning friends during his wife's battle with cancer. The couple endured several misguided attempts to provide comfort while she was ill. Some of the comments were along the lines of "You'll be glad you went through this one day" and "This is really a blessing in disguise." The couple found those comments to be dismissive and unhelpful. Rather, they came to appreciate this biblical counsel: "Weep with those who weep" (Romans 12:15). We support others when we acknowledge the legitimacy of their struggle and shoulder the load with them.

"With God's help, you'll get through this. You're going to make it." A distressed person needs to know that life goes on. One time, as I was feeling distraught after a negative experience, a wise mentor announced to me, "You can recover from this." He assured me there is a path forward.

As Christians, we call this phenomenon hope. God's Word says, "We rejoice in our sufferings, knowing that suffering produces endurance, and endurance produces character, and character produces hope, and hope does not put us to shame" (Romans 5:3–5). Hope does not put us to shame, because our hope is in God and not ourselves. Trials can lead us to greater dependence on God and consequently greater hope. In distress, we don't intuitively sense this. It needs to be announced.

You can do that for others. Announce that there is a path forward. *"God will give you the strength you need. The Lord is with you."* Words like these affirm God's faithfulness. Simple statements suffice. You don't have to expound eloquent theological treatises to affirm God's faithfulness. Simply reminding a struggling person that God is in the picture anchors them in faith. When we affirm God's faithfulness, we frame problems within a larger context. We remind others that it's all in God's hands.

"I'm praying for you." What an honor to be in someone's prayers. Think about it: when someone prays for you, they're including you in their conversation with the almighty Maker of heaven and earth! You can provide that assurance to others, informing them that you're lifting up their needs to God's heavenly throne. God's Word teaches us "the prayer of a righteous person has great power as it is working" (James 5:16). Prayer is powerful because the One who hears us is all powerful and graciously works for our good.

Spirit-Prompted Words

As you speak to the distressed, be emboldened by Jesus' promise: "The Holy Spirit will teach you in that very hour what you ought to say" (Luke 12:12). Jesus spoke these words to His disciples to prepare them for the day when they would be persecuted for their faith. Rather than fret about what to say, they could trust the Spirit to guide them.

The Spirit also is our guide as we speak to others. Sometimes we get nervous and worry, "What am I supposed to say?" Feeling inadequate, we shy away and provide no comfort. Trust the Holy Spirit to help you as you seek to encourage others. Bolstered by your faith in Christ, you're able to anchor others in faith. You're able to assure them that God is with them and at work for their good.

One time, a pastor and his son were having a conversation about God doing the impossible. That Sunday, the pastor preached about Jonah and the whale. Later at home, the pastor's young son asked about the likelihood of such an incredible story.

"Daddy, do you really believe that a fish could swallow a man and keep the man alive for three days and three nights?"

His father replied, "Son, if God could create a man out of nothing, and if God could create the first sea creature out of nothing, don't you think He would have the power to make a fish that could swallow a man and keep him alive for three days and three nights?"

The boy replied, "Well, if you're going to bring God into it, that's different!"

Through our words of encouragement, you and I have the joy of bringing God into it. We have the privilege of pointing others to the Lord, who calms troubled hearts and instills peace.

FOR DISCUSSION

1. All of us experience stress to some degree. What do you do to relieve stress?

2. How did it help Samuel when he acknowledged the problem?

3. On page 131, the author describes a portion of Samuel's message by saying, "The past was done. It was time to establish a new and better future." In what area of your life do you need to work toward change for the future? Envision what that preferred future might look like. Bring these hopes to God in prayer.

4. God honors His promises. What promises of God do you depend on most?

5. Samuel said it would be a sin not to pray for the people. What did he mean by that?

6. What comes to mind when you hear the word *repent*?

7. How has God shown Himself to be faithful in your life?

8. This chapter presents a four-part formula, based on Samuel's farewell address, to use when speaking to people in distress. Choose one of the four parts and explain why it's meaningful to you.

9. Have you ever felt that God gave you the words you needed to say in a certain situation? Share the experience.

Ps. 4:1

CHAPTER 11

Don't Panic!

(1 SAMUEL 13)

You have done foolishly. You have not kept the command of the LORD your God, with which He commanded you. For then the LORD would have established your kingdom over Israel forever. But now your kingdom shall not continue. The LORD has sought out a man after His own heart, and the LORD has commanded him to be prince over His people, because you have not kept what the LORD commanded you.

1 SAMUEL 13:13-14

Excuses. We speak them. We hear them. We shake our heads at them. Teachers encounter a lot of excuses. When the homework assignment isn't turned in, get ready for some creative explanations!

Some excuses butter up the teacher. "I didn't have time to complete the homework yesterday because I was at a rally all day. The rally was calling for an increase in teacher pay, so I had to be there!"

Some appeal to logic. "I figured I'd do my homework tomorrow, because I'll be older and therefore wiser!"

Some are the consequence of brilliance. "On yesterday's assignment, I did everything right, even the tasks for extra credit. Today, I couldn't find it, so I went to my mom. She had taken it to be professionally framed!"

And in today's digital age, when homework can be submitted electronically: "You didn't get my homework? Weird. I emailed it yesterday. Must have gotten lost in cyberspace."

Take responsibility? Nah! Self-exonerate? Yeah!

Saul Panics

No one appreciates hearing excuses. Samuel didn't.

Saul had overstepped his role as king. He had swerved out of his lane. Samuel was running late. Saul panicked. And in his panic, the king made a hasty decision with disastrous personal consequences.

The disaster took shape as the Israelite and Philistine armies positioned themselves for war.

The king's heart rate increased as he watched the enemy Philistine forces gathering in strength—"thirty thousand chariots and six thousand horsemen and troops like the sand on the seashore in multitude" (1 Samuel 13:5).

Saul's anxiety multiplied as he witnessed his soldiers shrinking in fear. Recognizing that "they were in trouble," the men of Israel "hid themselves in caves and in holes and in rocks and in tombs and in cisterns" (v. 6). Some fled. Those who remained with Saul "followed him trembling" (v. 7).

It was a pitiful scene. Saul watched as courage dissolved into terror. The mood was shifting rapidly to his disadvantage.

Where was Samuel? Nowhere to be found. He promised to be there in seven days. Saul waited seven days. Not seeing the prophet, the king took matters into his own hands.

Saul feared that without a priestly sacrifice, Israel would not be divinely favored in battle. So Saul did it himself. He offered a sacrifice. Big mistake. As the burnt offering went up in smoke, so did his long-term prospects as head of a royal line.

Acting in Haste

Saul panicked. Have you ever panicked and acted uncharacteristically? Times of change are ripe for hasty actions.

For example, a rule of thumb for dealing with grief is to wait at least a year before making any major life changes. In times of loss, we're not in a normal mental and emotional state. We're in a fog. Many times people initiate a major life change in an attempt to escape the pain of grief. Changes may include moving to a new house or a new city, changing jobs, making a significant purchase, dating, or marrying. Many relationships fail when they're little more than a rebound.

In most cases, it's advisable to wait until life stabilizes before making a major life change. There are exceptions, of course. But in most situations, it's wisest to wait for a life-shaking event to subside before committing to something new and significant.

Proverbs 19:2 teaches, "Desire without knowledge is not good, and whoever makes haste with his feet misses his way." When we rush, we can misstep and veer off in the wrong direction. Timing matters. Reasonable, carefully considered decisions often work out best.

Saul is a prime example of acting unwisely in the heat of the moment.

Not My Fault!

Right after Saul offered his unlawful sacrifice, guess who arrived? Samuel! The prophet immediately confronted the king: "What have you done?" (1 Samuel 13:11).

Saul responded with excuses: "When I saw that the people were scattering from me, and that you did not come within the days appointed, and that the Philistines had mustered at Michmash, I said, 'Now the Philistines will come down against me at Gilgal, and I have not sought the favor of the LORD.' So I forced myself, and offered the burnt offering" (vv. 11–12).

Saul made a mistake, but he refused to own it. He usurped the prophet's duties, but he denied responsibility. Instead, he rattled off excuses.

It's the people's fault. They were bailing on me.

It's your fault, Samuel. You were late.

It's the Philistines' fault. They were pressuring me.

I had no choice. I didn't want to do it.

He concluded his litany of blame by saying, "So I forced myself, and offered the burnt offering" (v. 12).

By his own account, he acted under compulsion, a victim of circumstances.

Why did Saul make excuses? Why do we make excuses? Excuses transfer the burden away from us. Excuses redirect attention. We want to avoid feeling guilty. None of us want to feel that we've come up short. Rather than admit wrongdoing, we deflect pain by shifting blame. Our first parents instituted the pattern: Adam blamed Eve, Eve blamed the serpent. The cycle continues.

God isn't fooled by excuses. He sees. He knows. All creation stands accountable before Him. Romans 1 teaches that God has revealed Himself through nature. Therefore, God declares of sinful humanity, "They are without excuse" (Romans 1:20). God holds those who know the truth to an even higher standard. Jesus said, "If I had not come and spoken to them, they would not have been guilty of sin, but now they have no excuses for their sin" (John 15:22).

Foolishness and Consequences

Samuel declared Saul's guilt by saying to the Lord's anointed, "You have done foolishly. You have not kept the command of the LORD your God, with which He commanded you. For then the LORD would have established your kingdom over Israel forever. But now your kingdom shall not continue. The LORD has sought out a man after His own heart, and the LORD has commanded him to be prince over His people, because you have not kept what the LORD commanded you" (1 Samuel 13:13–14).

The word *command*, or *commanded*, appears four times in those verses. What command had Saul violated? Samuel issued this command in 1 Samuel 10:8: "Then go down before me to Gilgal." (Saul did that.) "And behold, I am coming down to you to offer burnt offerings and to sacrifice peace offerings. Seven days you shall wait," (Saul did that) "until I come to you and show you what you shall do."

Oh. There's the problem. Saul waited seven days, but he didn't wait until Samuel came!

Just as our errant actions expose our sinful hearts, Saul's deeds revealed that his heart was not in the right place. Saul's trust in God faltered, and the king stumbled.

As a result, Samuel announced the consequences:

> But now your kingdom shall not continue. The LORD has sought out a man after His own heart, and the LORD has commanded him to be prince over His people, because you have not kept what the LORD commanded you.
> (1 Samuel 13:14)

God sought someone with a different heart. In the New Testament, Paul identified Saul's successor, David, as the man with the God-approved heart: "He raised up David to be their king, of whom He testified and said, 'I have found in David the son of Jesse a man after My heart, who will do all My will'" (Acts 13:22).

Accepting Responsibility for Us

David foreshadowed the perfect man after God's own heart: Jesus. Jesus' words and actions always aligned with His Father's will. Jesus never acted rashly or haphazardly, and He was never caught up in the moment. His actions were always measured, appropriate, and, most important, God-honoring.

The events leading to the cross demonstrated Jesus' focus and self-control. As He was beaten and harassed, He could have responded rashly by cursing His tormentors. Instead, when struck, He turned the other cheek. While under interrogation before the Jewish and Roman authorities, He could have impulsively answered every question thrown at Him. Instead, He spoke sparingly, only enough to identify Himself as the true King whose kingdom is not of this world.

On the cross, Jesus refrained from hasty behavior. The crowds teased Jesus to come down from the cross. The soldiers chimed in, saying, "If You are the King of the Jews, save Yourself!" (Luke 23:37). Pain was shooting through His body. Relief was possible. As the almighty Son of God, Jesus could have spared Himself. Legions of angels were on standby. Just a word from their Master would have activated them to perform a heavenly rescue mission (Matthew 26:53). Or, if He preferred, Jesus could have dismounted from the cross of His own accord.

But Jesus remained. For six long hours, He endured the cross. Unlike Saul, Jesus didn't offer a foolish sacrifice. Jesus was the sacrifice. He, the wisdom of God, chose the foolishness of the cross. Nothing deterred Him from His commitment to our salvation.

In Jesus' death, we see the Son of God accepting responsibility. Jesus accepted full responsibility for all of our wrongs. He did no wrong. But His tormentors did. They sinned. So do we. We sin against

God daily. We pile up a mountain of transgressions. But through the blood of Jesus, we are forgiven and set free.

Responding to Hasty Mistakes

Jesus' sacrifice sets the course for how we respond to our mistakes. Rather than deny our sins, we confess them. We hear God's words of forgiveness spoken over us and rejoice in His grace. From a church altar—which recalls the place of sacrifice—we receive the body and blood of our Savior as God's forgiveness comes to us in bread and wine connected with God's sanctifying Word.

Hear the Word of the Lord: "If we say we have no sin [excuses], we deceive ourselves, and the truth is not in us. If we confess our sins [taking responsibility], He is faithful and just to forgive us our sins and to cleanse us from all unrighteousness" (1 John 1:8–9).

As God's forgiven people, we move forward in His grace. Have you ever made a hasty decision and later regretted it? Read these words slowly and take them to heart: through Jesus, God forgives us.

He forgives *you*.

One time, a husband and wife were struggling through a rocky season in their marriage. There was one argument after another. They were committed to making their marriage work and agreed on an idea. They each made a box with an opening at the top. Each time they were frustrated with the other person, instead of sounding off in the moment, they wrote the complaint and put it in the box.

At the end of the month, they exchanged boxes. The husband opened his box and read the grievances: wet towel on the floor, forgot to take out the trash, got home late and didn't call ahead.

Then the wife opened her box and began reading. The first paper simply said, "I love you."

The next was the same: "I love you."

She pulled out every slip of paper, and they all had the same three words: "I love you." "I love you." "I love you."

No matter how much you mess up, God's message to you is always the same. Through the cross, God says, "I love you." He doesn't hold your sins against you. His love for you is greater than your sins.

FOR DISCUSSION

1. Saul acted in haste. Share a time when you acted in haste. What was the result?

2. Read Proverbs 19:2. How does acting in haste cause us to miss our way?

3. How do you think Saul felt when Samuel announced that his "kingdom shall not continue" (1 Samuel 13:14)? What thoughts might have gone through Saul's mind?

4. Why are we often inclined to deny our sins rather than confess them?

5. Jesus accepted full responsibility for all our wrongs. How do you feel upon reading those words?

6. On page 147, the author writes, "As God's forgiven people, we move forward in His grace." How does God's grace help us move forward?

7. A beloved verse on God's plans is Jeremiah 29:11. Share a time when you saw God accomplish good in your life in spite of a mistake you or someone else made.

8. Rather than act in haste, brainstorm ways you can slow down and handle life at a more manageable pace. Then, spend some time in prayer, asking God to help you with the pacing of life.

CHAPTER 12

Changes Can Change

(1 SAMUEL 15)

As Samuel turned to go away, Saul seized the skirt of his robe, and tore it. And Samuel said to him, "The LORD has torn the kingdom of Israel from you this day and has given it to a neighbor of yours, who is better than you."

1 SAMUEL 15:27–28

In our nation's history, we've had forty-six presidents, as of this writing. Thirteen have served two terms (or more, in the case of Franklin Roosevelt, who was elected president four times). Some presidents have stepped down after one term. Some have died in office. And some have run for reelection and lost. To be exact, ten have been one-term presidents.

Think about it. In one year, a candidate was so popular that he was elected to the nation's highest office. Four years later, he was voted out in favor of someone else. At one time, upon election, *he* was the change people wanted to see. Four years later, he was traded out for someone new.

Changes can change. This reality is a two-sided coin: good news for some and bad news for others.

Saul's Second Big Mistake

For Saul, a change in leadership was bad news. He was being traded out for someone new. The first kingship of Israel started out auspiciously for Saul but fell apart rapidly.

We read in the previous chapter about Saul's critical mistake in usurping the prophet's authority. By disregarding Samuel's role, Saul was disobeying God and His ultimate authority. The king panicked and acted rashly. The consequences were dire—God rejected Saul as king.

Two chapters later, the king committed a second foolish act that reinforced God's decision to oust Saul. Samuel delivered a divine order to Saul. Per almighty God, the king was to lead his army into battle against the Amalekites. The prophet explicitly instructed the king to "devote to destruction all that they have" (1 Samuel 15:3), which included all people and animals.

All. Every last one.

This is a tough directive to read. If a human being had ordered the destruction of an entire nation, we might deem such military warfare to be excessive and inhumane, a war crime of historic proportions. But when the order comes from God, we have to look at it differently. God's thoughts are above our thoughts, and His ways are above our ways (see Isaiah 55:8). His judgments are always just (see Deuteronomy 32:4).

Commenting on the order to annihilate in 1 Samuel 15:3, *The Lutheran Study Bible* explains it this way: "For ancient Israel, it was God's way of giving His people the land He had promised them and taking it from a people who for centuries had turned their backs on God and engaged in the vilest practices."

In His perfect justice, God issued the order, spoken through the prophet. There was no turning back from God's Word. Saul had two options: obey or disobey. And again he chose wrong. "But Saul and the people spared Agag [the king of the Amalekites] and the best of the sheep and of the oxen and of the fattened calves and the lambs, and all that was good, and would not utterly destroy them" (1 Samuel 15:9).

When the prophet confronted Saul, the king again pointed at others. He said the people pressured him. He insisted that he had obeyed God . . . mostly. The king rationalized his disobedience, claiming he preserved the choice animals to sacrifice them to the Lord.

Samuel stood his ground. He informed the king that "to obey is better than sacrifice" (15:22). A sacrifice out of disobedience does not satisfy the Lord.

After Saul's unlawful sacrifice, noted in 1 Samuel 13, the prophet announced that God was looking for a new king to replace Saul. In chapter 15, the prophet responded to the king's insubordination with a blunt declaration: "You have rejected the word of the LORD, and the LORD has rejected you from being king over Israel" (1 Samuel 15:26).

At those words, the prophet pivoted and began to walk away. Saul tried to stop Samuel. The king grabbed the prophet's robe. The robe ripped. The irony was unmistakable. Samuel let the truth sink in, saying to the king, "The LORD has torn the kingdom of Israel from you this day and has given it to a neighbor of yours, who is better than you" (v. 28).

At one time, Saul was the change. Now he was being changed out for a new king.

A Wandering Heart

In his Large Catechism, Luther noted Saul as an example of someone who trusted in his own power instead of God's. Commenting on the First Commandment, Luther wrote, "Saul was a great king, chosen by God, and a godly man. But when he was established on his throne, he let his heart wander from God and put his trust in his crown and power [1 Samuel 9–13]" (Large Catechism, Part 1, paragraph 45).

In Saul's latest act of disobedience, how do we see that the king's heart wandered from God?

First, Saul tried to improve on God's Word. God gave a specific commandment through the prophet—destroy all. Saul tried to modify the commandment to suit his preferences. Killing the choicest animals should have taken place in war, not afterward on an altar.

Do we ever do that? Do we ever twist God's Word to make it fit our preferences? For catechism class one day, we watched a video about ways *not* to pray. Most of them were humorous. One way *not* to pray is gossip disguised as prayer requests. The Eighth Commandment forbids any speech that harms our neighbor's reputation. Do we ever share personal information about others because "he needs prayer *badly*"? We "baptize" our gossip by treating it as a prayer request. But it's still gossip, harmful to our neighbor's reputation. That's one example of trying to circumvent God's Word according to our sinful inclinations.

Second, Saul failed to acknowledge his sin . . . until the prophet painted the king into an inescapable corner of truth. When first confronted, the king blamed his soldiers. He insisted that his actions were above reproach. Any misdeed came from the troops on the ground, not the supervising commander.

Many of us are experts at the blame game. When we make a mistake, we don't want to be under the hot spotlight of truth. We'd rather shift the attention elsewhere and spare ourselves the discomfort of honest confession.

As sinful people, we, too, drift from God in our thoughts, words, and deeds. The hymn "Come, Thou Fount of Every Blessing" says it well: "Prone to wander, Lord, I feel it; Prone to leave the God I love" (*LSB* 686:1). Like Saul, our heart can stray from God and His ways.

Saul put his trust in his crown and power. We put our trust in whatever makes us feel strong and self-sufficient—positions, accomplishments, money, possessions, degrees. Putting too much stock in the things of this world didn't work for Saul. It doesn't work for us either. At some point, we hit a wall, and the only remedy is to return to the Lord, seeking His mercy.

The Heir of Saul's Successor

Thankfully, God took the initiative to reconcile fallen humanity to Himself. Out of the royal family that succeeded Saul, God provided a Savior who loves us, forgives us, and restores us to God. In that sense, bad news for Saul became good news for the human race.

Saul's successor was David, and David's heir was Jesus Christ. Jesus is the King whose dominion endures forever. And He's a very different kind of king. While on trial before Pontius Pilate, Jesus said, "My kingdom is not of this world" (John 18:36). Jesus was not driven by worldly values but by a heavenly agenda. The salvation of humankind motivated our true King to come into this world in lowliness.

Unlike earthly kings, Jesus didn't take power but gave up His power. In 1 Samuel 8, Samuel warned the people that an earthly king would be a taker. "He will take your sons. . . . He will take your daughters. . . . He will take the best of your fields. . . . He will take the tenth of your grain. . . . He will take your male servants and female servants. . . . He will take the tenth of your flocks" (1 Samuel 8:11–17a). Ultimately the king would take their freedom: "And you shall be his slaves" (v. 17b). Because of our sinful nature, we, too, can be takers, asking "What can I get?" instead of "What can I give?"

Jesus was different. He willingly humbled Himself. He "emptied Himself, by taking on the form of a servant" (Philippians 2:7). Our King, Jesus, didn't stand over people and dominate them. He placed Himself beneath others, washed their feet, cared for their needs, and served selflessly. Jesus is the ultimate giver.

Unlike earthly kings, Jesus didn't hoard riches but gave His riches away. "For you know the grace of our Lord Jesus Christ, that though He was rich, yet for your sakes He became poor, so that you by His poverty might become rich" (2 Corinthians 8:9). He had it all! He was in heaven, worshiped by the angels and saints. Then He left His heavenly throne and became an embryo in His mother's womb.

Through His poverty, we became rich. He gave Himself for us so that we would have "treasures in heaven, where neither moth nor rust destroys and where thieves do not break in and steal" (Matthew 6:20). The riches of kings and peasants alike fade away, but the treasures that are ours in Christ are permanent, an eternal inheritance.

Unlike earthly kings, Jesus didn't take life but gave His life on the cross so all who believe in Him could have life forevermore. Even good kings like David gained notoriety for taking life. While Saul was still alive and David was king-in-waiting, a popular chant arose: "Saul has struck down his thousands, and David his ten thousands" (1 Samuel 18:7). Successful kings took life.

Not Jesus. He harmed no one. Matthew applied these words of the prophet Isaiah to Jesus, the Servant-King: "A bruised reed He will not break, and a faintly burning wick He will not quench" (Isaiah 42:3; Matthew 12:20). Jesus didn't come to break people. He came to restore us to fullness before our heavenly Father. He accomplished this objective through the cross, where He paid the ultimate price for our sins. He gave His life in exchange for ours. The mighty King died for His lowly subjects, sinners like you and me.

Jesus is a one-of-a-kind King.

The New You

Through Jesus, one king is exchanged for another. By faith, the king of "me" is dethroned, and Christ sits on the throne of our hearts. Our sinful nature is drowned in the waters of Baptism, and a new person arises, filled with God's Spirit and empowered for service in His name. Out with the old, in with the new! "Therefore, if anyone is in Christ, he is a new creation. The old has passed away; behold, the new has come" (2 Corinthians 5:17).

Through Jesus, a radical change takes place in us. Sinners become saints. Transgressors are transformed. Rascals are made righteous. The irredeemable are redeemed. Purchased by Christ's blood, you are what God declares you to be: a new creation in Christ!

A story has been told about the great French general Napoleon. One day, a young private rode in quickly on horseback to bring the general important news. The general was impressed with the young private's detailed report. Napoleon said to him, "Thank you, Captain."

And from that moment on, the young man was no longer a private. He had a new rank: captain. How? Did he go through months of training? Did he pass through a process of promotion? No. The general declared him to be a captain, and so he was.

God has declared you to be a new creation in Christ, and so you are! You're not captive to your sinful nature; you are set free. You're not subject to the dictates of our fallen world; you live under the gracious rule of our heavenly King.

Do some old habits still cling to you? With God's Spirit living in you, He empowers you to live your new life in Christ and put the old self behind you!

Frustrated by mistake after mistake? Through Word and Sacrament, God's power pulses in your veins, enabling you to reject what's wrong and choose what's right!

Eager for change in your life? With God's help, a personal reformation is possible as He continues to produce growth and maturity in you day by day!

"For the grace of God has appeared, bringing salvation to all people, training us to renounce ungodliness and worldly passions, and to live self-controlled, upright, and godly lives in the present age" (Titus 2:11–12).

The kingdom was torn away from Saul. What God gives you in Jesus can never be taken away. God's forgiveness, His grace, His love—these are yours now and forever!

FOR DISCUSSION

1. How do you typically react to instructions given to you? Do you obey readily? insist on understanding why before you act? try to find a way out of the task? give some other response?

2. Why do you think Saul disobeyed the command to exterminate the enemy?

3. Read Isaiah 55:8. How does this verse help us as we wrestle with difficult passages, like God's order to Saul to destroy the Amalekites?

4. Samuel confronted Saul with his sin. On a scale of one (easy) to ten (difficult), how difficult is it for you to confront people?

5. When someone confronts you, what is your typical response? Are you more likely to accept the person's point of view, or are you more likely to get defensive?

6. According to Luther, Saul's downfall was because he "put his trust in his crown and power." When are you tempted to put your trust in yourself instead of in God? For you, what strengths create an illusion of self-sufficiency?

7. Read Titus 2:11–12. What does it look like to "renounce ungodliness and worldly passions"?

8. What does it look like to "live self-controlled, upright, and godly lives"?

9. Saul followed God's command . . . partly. How can you walk in greater obedience to the Lord this week?

CHAPTER 13

Moving Forward with God

(1 SAMUEL 16)

> The LORD said to Samuel, "How long
> will you grieve over Saul, since I have
> rejected him from being king over Israel?
> Fill your horn with oil, and go."
>
> 1 SAMUEL 16:1

One of the most successful outreach ministries in the congregation I serve is our grief support ministry. The program is a wonderful, Scripture-based curriculum that covers a wide range of topics related to grief. About 80 percent of those who attend are not members of the church. The program meets a universal need—the need to deal with grief in a healthy way.

Our program facilitator, Mark, began leading the group after his wife passed away suddenly. Having journeyed through intense grief himself, Mark wanted to help others on that same heart-wrenching path. After each new group, Mark sends me a report of how many participated, and he also provides me with feedback cards from group members. Without fail, the feedback is overwhelmingly positive. Many participants will testify that they come in feeling lost and leave with renewed hope and purpose.

One person wrote succinctly on a comment card, "Thank you. I'm grateful this space exists. Moving forward, I'm not feeling so alone."

Two of those words deserve special notice: "moving forward." That's the key. We don't want to stay stuck in grief. We want to move forward. By God's grace, we can.

Samuel's Grief

Grief isn't only about the death of a loved one. We can also grieve over the death of a dream or the end of how things used to be or the conclusion of a special chapter in life.

Samuel felt profound grief over how things turned out with Saul. First, the prophet was saddened when people rejected God as their king—and rejected Samuel and his sons. Then, once Saul was established as king, Samuel watched in horror as the king's sinfulness resulted in not one but two tragic decisions. As a result of those decisions, the Lord deemed Saul unfit to head a royal line.

It wasn't supposed to go that way! But it did. And the prophet was struggling with feelings of sadness.

First Samuel 16 opens with these words: "The LORD said to Samuel, 'How long will you grieve over Saul, since I have rejected him from being king over Israel?'" (1 Samuel 16:1a).

Implied in those words: *Samuel, you've grieved long enough. The decision is final. There's no going back. Time to move forward.*

God, in His mercy, didn't leave Samuel to figure out how to move forward. The Lord made it clear with His next words. "Fill your horn with oil, and go. I will send you to Jesse the Bethlehemite, for I have provided for Myself a king from among his sons" (v. 1b).

God told Samuel, "Go."

Do you need to hear that two-letter word?

Go!

You and I can get stuck. We can get stuck mentally. Sometimes we have a hard time moving past whatever we're grieving. I'll admit it happens to me. At times it can be almost debilitating. I can recall seasons of disappointment when I was stuck in the past, rehashing painful moments in my mind. The events had long since passed, but in my mind, they were fresh. Imprisoned by memories and feelings, I'd become stuck.

One time in my stuck-ness, a wise mentor said to me bluntly yet compassionately, "You have to let it go." There's that two-letter word again: go. Let it go and go forward.

A New King

God had a plan for His people and for Samuel. The plan wasn't for the prophet and the nation to be stuck. The plan was to move forward, to turn the page to a new and better chapter.

God sent Samuel to a man named Jesse, who had several sons. After meeting Jesse and his sons, Samuel knew the future king of Israel was standing before him. His name was . . . Eliab.

Yes, Samuel had it wrong.

God said to Samuel, "Do not look on his appearance or on the height of his stature, because I have rejected him. For the LORD sees not as man sees: man looks on the outward appearance, but the LORD looks on the heart" (1 Samuel 16:7).

What wonderful assurance! The world may judge us by outward appearances—physique, fashion, personal charm—but God looks deeper. His eye sees what's on the inside. The heart matters most to God.

With this framework in mind, Samuel watched as one son after another paraded past him. The verdict was clear for each: "Neither has the LORD chosen this one" (vv. 8–9).

After seven of Jesse's sons failed to pass the test, Samuel asked Jesse if he had any more sons. Jesse said one son remained, the youngest, who was out tending sheep. Jesse summoned his youngest son. After Samuel saw the boy, the voice of the Lord pronounced, "Arise, anoint him, for this is he" (v. 12).

Samuel obediently anointed the youngest with oil in front of his brothers. "And the Spirit of the LORD rushed upon David from that day forward" (v. 13).

If Samuel had been paralyzed by grief over Saul, the prophet never would have discovered the next king. But at God's instruction, Samuel moved forward. He left the past behind him and stepped boldly into a new and better future. He anointed the new king, whose line would one day produce the King of kings.

God revealed His plan for David's line when He said, "Your house and your kingdom shall be made sure forever before Me. Your throne will be established forever" (2 Samuel 7:16).

David

It's hard to overstate David's importance in the story of salvation. Aside from God, David's name is the most prominent in all of Scripture! The name *David* appears 1,094 times in the Bible. By comparison, the name *Moses* appears 852 times, *Abraham* appears 239 times, *Paul* appears 162 times, and *Peter* appears 153 times. Samuel is named 142 times. The name *David* even appears more frequently than the name *Jesus* (966 occurrences).[13]

In David, we see God's grace. If his father, Jesse, had had his way, one of David's older brothers would have been selected as the Lord's

---

13   Number of occurrences comes from the ESV translation as listed on blueletterbible.org.

anointed. David, the youngest and smallest, was out tending sheep. But David was God's choice. By grace, God called David out of the pasture and into the office of king-designate.

In David, we see God's gift of faith. "The LORD looks on the heart" (1 Samuel 16:7). And the heart he saw in David was filled with faith. David trusted in God, a trust that God instilled in David through the working of the Holy Spirit. By faith, David stood up to Goliath and triumphed (see 1 Samuel 17). By faith, David inquired of God before attacking the Philistines (1 Samuel 23). By faith, David honored God's decisions, twice refusing to kill Saul when he had a chance. David refused because Saul was the Lord's anointed, and David submitted himself to God's judgments (see 1 Samuel 24; 26). By faith, David repented of his sins and relied on God's forgiveness (see 2 Samuel 12:13; 24:10). And if you really want an inside look into David's faith, read some of the seventy-three psalms he wrote. Most famous is Psalm 23, in which he declares, "The LORD is my shepherd" (Psalm 23:1).

In David, we see God's faithfulness. God remained true to His Word. He preserved a royal line for David. God cut off Saul's family line from the throne, but David's family maintained its high status. From 1 Samuel through the end of the Old Testament Historical Books, a descendant of David was recognized as the ruler of God's people. From David's son Solomon to the final Davidic leader of the Old Testament, Zerubbabel, the royal line continued.

In David's promised Son, we see God's gift of a Savior. God's greatest gift arrived about a thousand years after David when Jesus was born!

Son of David

Israel's new hope—King David—pointed ahead to the One who brought hope for all humankind, Jesus.

Fittingly, shepherds were the first to hear the good news of the Messiah's birth when an angel announced to them, "For unto you is born this day in the city of David a Savior, who is Christ the Lord" (Luke 2:11). The city of David was Bethlehem. The birthplace of Israel's most famous king was the birthplace of Israel's true King, Jesus. Even people who debated Jesus' identity uttered this truth: "Has not the Scripture said that the Christ comes from the offspring of David, and comes from Bethlehem, the village where David was?" (John 7:42).

The Gospel writers particularly emphasized Jesus' lineage from David. Matthew connected the dots when he introduced his Gospel as "the book of the genealogy of Jesus Christ, the son of David, the son of Abraham" (Matthew 1:1). The angel Gabriel told Mary, "The Lord God will give to Him the throne of His father David" (Luke 1:32). People desperate for healing cried out to Him, "Have mercy on us, Son of David" (Matthew 9:27). The crowds marveled at Jesus, asking, "Can this be the Son of David?" (Matthew 12:23). On Palm Sunday, as Jesus rode into Jerusalem, onlookers shouted, "Hosanna to the Son of David!" (Matthew 21:9).

Through David, God displaced an erring king, Saul. Through David's descendant, Jesus, God overthrew all imposters to the throne. "He disarmed the rulers and authorities and put them to open shame, by triumphing over them in Him" (Colossians 2:15).

With a crown of thorns, raised up on the throne of the cross, Jesus established God's reign for all time by defeating sin and death. In His resurrection, the King stood triumphant over His enemies, and He gives the victory to all who trust in Him.

A Walk of Grief

This victory, however, was in doubt before it was believed. On Easter Sunday, two disciples were walking to a town called Emmaus. Scripture names one—Cleopas—and leaves the other unnamed.

A third person, the resurrected Jesus, joined them on their walk. "But their eyes were kept from recognizing Him" (Luke 24:16). So they journeyed onward with their new friend. When Jesus asked what they were discussing, "they stood still, looking sad" (v. 17).

Why were they sad? They didn't know the good news! They didn't know that Jesus had risen from the dead. As far as they knew, Jesus had been killed on the cross and that was the end of the story. They presumed—reasonably—that His body was in a grave; dead people tend to remain dead!

They recounted to Jesus the events of the past couple of days, centering around Jesus' condemnation and execution. They said, "But we had hoped He was the one to redeem Israel" (v. 21).

Do you hear the grief? *We had hoped.* The death of a dream. An unrealized expectation.

They weren't just walking down a road to a town. They were walking down a path called grief.

But they didn't stay in their grief. What moved them forward? The good news of the resurrection! While they were walking, Jesus "interpreted to them in all the Scriptures the things concerning Himself" (v. 27). Then, as they drew near to the village, the two disciples urged Jesus to stay with them. So He stayed and ate dinner with them. As they broke bread together, "their eyes were opened, and they recognized Him" (v. 31).

Can you imagine their surprise? What joy must have filled their hearts!

Later they found the eleven disciples and shared the good news: "The Lord has risen indeed, and has appeared to Simon!" (v. 34).

Christ's resurrection transformed their grief into joy. His resurrection does the same for us. The death of a loved one can be devastating. We find comfort in knowing that the souls of believers are with the Lord. And our joy increases when we celebrate the promise that "in Christ shall all be made alive" (1 Corinthians 15:22). With eager expectation, we anticipate the day when Christ will return in glory and "God will bring with Him those who have fallen asleep" (1 Thessalonians 4:14).

Without the good news of the resurrection, the disciples traveling to Emmaus were trapped in sadness. But once they knew that Jesus had risen, their hearts were overcome with joy.

How many people all around us are unaware of the Good News of Jesus? So many people are lost in sadness, not knowing where to turn or how to move forward. We have the message of life. Pray that God would open our lips to tell of His goodness so that others may believe and find comfort in the hope of eternal life in Christ!

Envisioning a Better Future

Through our faith, God gives us hope to press forward in the face of grief. Whether you're grieving the loss of a loved one, a dream, a season of life, or something else, you can find comfort in the presence and promise of your Savior, Jesus. He had a plan for your life. His plan never comes to a standstill. He is always leading us forward. He is always moving us ahead to the next chapter.

With God, there's always a next chapter. It may not be like the previous chapter, but God is still writing your life story. And He is a skilled author whose work is always good.

Rev. Michael W. Newman wrote a wonderful book titled *Hope When Your Heart Breaks: Navigating Grief and Loss.* In his closing chapter, he offers a compelling vision for life after heartbreak:

> One day, you'll not only feel normal again, but you'll be excited about something. You'll be able to look back at your grief without crying—at least once in a while. You may even see a glimpse of God's purpose in your pain.
>
> When that happens, you'll know that your grief companion is being tired out and worn down by God's tenacious help and healing. You'll realize that God has

been chasing after you, pursuing you with determination
and unrelenting love. Heartbreak will always be hang-
ing around somewhere, but instead of being overcome
with anguish, you'll be filled with wisdom and compassion. You will possess a new spirit of empathy and will
approach people with patient understanding. Your heart
will no longer be torn by grief but seasoned by it. You will
sense a new beginning.[14]

In the midst of grief, that's what we need: a vision for a better
future. God doesn't want us to be stuck in grief. In love, He sent a
Savior to rescue us from sin and sadness. Faith in Christ gives us a
fresh, compelling vision that leads us forward in hope and victory.

My two oldest boys love sports. They love to play sports and
watch sports. When they watch sports, they consider themselves
part of their favorite team. When the team scores, the boys will say,
"We scored!" When the team wins, they'll celebrate—"We won!"
Did they shoot the ball into the hoop? No. Did they run into the
end zone? No. But they identify so closely with their team that they
claim the team's victory as their own.

Because Jesus has overcome, we overcome too. Some days, you
may not feel like an overcomer. You might feel depressed, lost in
the wilderness, stuck in a dark place. The victory is not based on
our feelings or experiences. It's based on Jesus' actions. He died on
the cross for our sins and rose from the grave triumphant. In this
world, we will struggle. But He has overcome the world. By faith,
His victory is ours!

---

14   Michael W. Newman, *Hope When Your Heart Breaks: Navigating Grief and Loss* (St.
      Louis: Concordia Publishing House, 2017), 214.

FOR DISCUSSION

1. If you were giving someone advice about grief, what would you say?

2. Are you grieving anything right now? Share if you're comfortable doing so.

3. Why was Samuel grieving over Saul?

4. What causes you to feel stuck? What helps you to get unstuck?

5. In what area of life do you need to hear "Go"?

6. The Bible describes David as a man after God's own heart (see 1 Samuel 13:14; Acts 13:22). What do you think the Lord saw in David's heart?

7. How does Christ's resurrection transform grief into joy?

8. Reread the quote from Pastor Newman. What is the quote saying to you about moving forward?

9. In the midst of grief, we need a vision for a better future. Cast a vision for a better future for you, a future built on hope in the Lord's ability to work out good in your life. What is included in that vision?

Conclusion

With David's anointing as king, Samuel stepped aside, and the spotlight shined brightly on David from then onward. The prophet receives mention only a few more times in 1 Samuel. In a weird scene, Saul stripped naked and prophesied in front of Samuel all day and all night (see 1 Samuel 19). In an even more bizarre and confusing scene after Samuel's death, a witch summoned Samuel's spirit (or possibly an evil spirit posing as Samuel) to speak to Saul (see 1 Samuel 28).

The Bible describes Samuel's death in 1 Samuel 25:1, saying, "All Israel assembled and mourned for him, and they buried him in his house in Ramah."

The narrative of Samuel's life is contained in 1 Samuel. Outside of the first book bearing his name, Samuel is mentioned most often in 1 and 2 Chronicles. These books of the Bible recap much of what is in the books of Samuel and Kings but with additional information. As we read earlier, Samuel's sons didn't turn out well, but his grandson Heman was a skilled musician who sang and played cymbals and possibly other instruments (see 1 Chronicles 6:33; 15:19).

Samuel was actively involved in the administration of the tabernacle. He and David jointly appointed gatekeepers (see 1 Chronicles 9:22). He dedicated gifts for the maintenance of God's house (see 1 Chronicles 26:28). Under Samuel's leadership, the Passover festival of his day was heralded as one of the greatest in Israel's history (see 2 Chronicles 35:18).

The great prophet also was an accomplished writer. He composed a volume of the acts of King David (see 1 Chronicles 29:29).

The New Testament highlights Samuel as the last judge (see Acts 13:20) and the first of the prophets (see Acts 3:24).

Samuel is enshrined in the Hebrews 11 "Hall of Faith," although it feels like the writer is moving through the verse quickly so he can get to the greater point. "And what more shall I say? For time would fail me to tell of Gideon, Barak, Samson, Jephthah, of David and Samuel and the prophets" (Hebrews 11:32).

Hebrews 11 is a strategic lead-up to chapter 12, the greater message:

> Therefore, since we are surrounded by so great a cloud of witnesses, let us also lay aside every weight, and sin which clings so closely, and let us run with endurance the race that is set before us, looking to Jesus, the founder and perfecter of our faith. (Hebrews 12:1–2)

Ultimately, that's what Samuel is—part of a great cloud of witnesses who preceded Jesus. Along with the other witnesses of Scripture, Samuel's life inspires us to lay aside every weight and sin and to run with endurance the race set before us. The race will have its twists and turns. Satan will try to derail us. The world will do its best to discourage us and convince us the Christian race isn't worth the trouble.

But by God's grace, we can run with endurance. God's Spirit strengthens us. God's Word directs us. A great cloud of witnesses, including Samuel, surrounds us. And our Savior stands victorious for us, over every change and loss, over every trouble and heartache, over every challenge and mountain that we may have to climb. Jesus stands triumphant over it all, and He invites us to journey with Him, filled with faith, hope, and joy.

God's Unfailing Words of Assurance

Change can stir up many different feelings. However you may feel, here are some reminders of God's care for you.

OUT OF CONTROL

Change reminds us that we have less control over our lives than we wish we had. When you feel out of control, reflect on the following verses:

> The LORD of hosts has sworn: "As I have planned, so shall it be, and as I have purposed, so shall it stand." (Isaiah 14:24)

> That people may know, from the rising of the sun and from the west, that there is none besides me; I am the LORD, and there is no other. I form light and create darkness; I make well-being and create calamity; I am the LORD, who does all these things. (Isaiah 45:6–7)

> Many are the plans in the mind of a man, but it is the purpose of the LORD that will stand. (Proverbs 19:21)

> The heart of man plans his way, but the LORD establishes his steps. (Proverbs 16:9)

> For I know the plans I have for you, declares the LORD, plans for welfare and not for evil, to give you a future and a hope. (Jeremiah 29:11)

Come now, you who say, "Today or tomorrow we will go into such and such a town and spend a year there and trade and make a profit"—yet you do not know what tomorrow will bring. What is your life? For you are a mist that appears for a little time and then vanishes. Instead you ought to say, "If the Lord wills, we will live and do this or that." (James 4:13-15)

And we know that for those who love God all things work together for good, for those who are called according to His purpose. (Romans 8:28)

Have I not commanded you? Be strong and courageous. Do not be frightened, and do not be dismayed, for the LORD your God is with you wherever you go. (Joshua 1:9)

ANXIOUS

We're not sure what's coming next, and that produces worry and fear. When anxiety plagues you, reflect on the following verses:

I have said these things to you, that in Me you may have peace. In the world you will have tribulation. But take heart; I have overcome the world. (John 16:33)

When the cares of my heart are many, Your consolations cheer my soul. (Psalm 94:19)

Peace I leave with you; My peace I give to you. Not as the world gives do I give to you. Let not your hearts be troubled, neither let them be afraid. (John 14:27)

Therefore do not be anxious about tomorrow, for tomorrow will be anxious for itself. Sufficient for the day is its own trouble. (Matthew 6:34)

It is in vain that you rise up early and go late to rest, eating the bread of anxious toil; for He gives to His beloved sleep. (Psalm 127:2)

And which of you by being anxious can add a single hour to his span of life? (Luke 12:25)

Humble yourselves, therefore, under the mighty hand of God so that at the proper time He may exalt you, casting all your anxieties on Him, because He cares for you. (1 Peter 5:6–7)

For God gave us a spirit not of fear but of power and love and self-control. (2 Timothy 1:7)

There is no fear in love, but perfect love casts out fear. For fear has to do with punishment, and whoever fears has not been perfected in love. (1 John 4:18)

Do not be anxious about anything, but in everything by prayer and supplication with thanksgiving let your requests be made known to God. And the peace of God, which surpasses all understanding, will guard your hearts and your minds in Christ Jesus. (Philippians 4:6–7)

SAD

The loss of a loved one is among the most difficult types of grief. When your spirit is in a valley of sadness, reflect on the following verses:

Blessed are those who mourn, for they shall be comforted. (Matthew 5:4)

He will wipe away every tear from their eyes, and death shall be no more, neither shall there be mourning, nor crying, nor pain anymore, for the former things have passed away. (Revelation 21:4)

He heals the brokenhearted and binds up their wounds. (Psalm 147:3)

The LORD is near to the brokenhearted and saves the crushed in spirit. (Psalm 34:18)

IRRELEVANT

You used to know the lay of the land, but things have changed, and now you're feeling left out. When you question whether you matter anymore, reflect on the following verses:

O LORD, You have searched me and known me! You know when I sit down and when I rise up; You discern my thoughts from afar. You search out my path and my lying down and are acquainted with all my ways. Even before a word is on my tongue, behold, O LORD, You know it altogether. You hem me in, behind and before, and lay Your hand upon me. (Psalm 139:1–5)

For God so loved the world, that He gave His only Son, that whoever believes in Him should not perish but have eternal life. (John 3:16)

In Him you also, when you heard the word of truth, the gospel of your salvation, and believed in Him, were sealed with the promised Holy Spirit, who is the guarantee of our inheritance until we acquire possession of it, to the praise of His glory. (Ephesians 1:13–14)

Are not two sparrows sold for a penny? And not one of them will fall to the ground apart from your Father. But even the hairs of your head are all numbered. Fear not, therefore; you are of more value than many sparrows. (Matthew 10:29–31)

But God shows His love for us in that while we were still sinners, Christ died for us. (Romans 5:8)

For You formed my inward parts; You knitted me together in my mother's womb. I praise You, for I am fearfully and wonderfully made. Wonderful are Your works; my soul knows it very well. My frame was not hidden from You, when I was being made in secret, intricately woven in the depths of the earth. (Psalm 139:13–15)

For we are His workmanship, created in Christ Jesus for good works, which God prepared beforehand, that we should walk in them. (Ephesians 2:10)

The LORD will fulfill His purpose for me; Your steadfast love, O LORD, endures forever. Do not forsake the work of Your hands. (Psalm 138:8)

But you are a chosen race, a royal priesthood, a holy nation, a people for His own possession, that you may proclaim the excellencies of Him who called you out of darkness into His marvelous light. (1 Peter 2:9)

PERPLEXED

In the midst of change, we can feel confused, struggling to find our place in a new normal. When you feel perplexed, reflect on the following verses:

Let my cry come before You, O Lᴏʀᴅ; give me understanding according to Your word! (Psalm 119:169)

Give me understanding, that I may keep Your law and observe it with my whole heart. (Psalm 119:34)

When the Spirit of truth comes, He will guide you into all the truth, for He will not speak on His own authority, but whatever He hears He will speak, and He will declare to you the things that are to come. (John 16:13)

We are afflicted in every way, but not crushed; perplexed, but not driven to despair. (2 Corinthians 4:8)

Trust in the Lᴏʀᴅ with all your heart, and do not lean on your own understanding. In all your ways acknowledge Him, and He will make straight your paths. (Proverbs 3:5–6)

UNSUPPORTED

Change can disrupt our network of family and friends. When you feel like you're all alone, reflect on the following verses:

Behold, God is my helper; the Lord is the upholder of my life. (Psalm 54:4)

So we can confidently say, "The Lord is my helper; I will not fear; what can man do to me?" (Hebrews 13:6)

But they who wait for the Lᴏʀᴅ shall renew their strength; they shall mount up with wings like eagles; they shall run and not be weary; they shall walk and not faint. (Isaiah 40:31)

And Asa cried to the Lᴏʀᴅ his God, "O Lᴏʀᴅ, there is none like You to help, between the mighty and the weak.

Help us, O Lord our God, for we rely on You, and in Your
name we have come against this multitude. O Lord,
You are our God; let not man prevail against You."
(2 Chronicles 14:11)

Cast your burden on the Lord, and He will sustain
you; He will never permit the righteous to be moved.
(Psalm 55:22)

Fear not, for I am with you; be not dismayed, for I am
your God; I will strengthen you, I will help you, I will
uphold you with My righteous right hand. (Isaiah 41:10)

I can do all things through Him who strengthens me.
(Philippians 4:13)

God is our refuge and strength, a very present help in
trouble. (Psalm 46:1)

Let us then with confidence draw near to the throne of
grace, that we may receive mercy and find grace to help
in time of need. (Hebrews 4:16)

OVERWHELMED

Sometimes life changes at a faster pace than we can keep up with.
When you feel overwhelmed, reflect on the following verses:

Therefore, since we are surrounded by so great a cloud
of witnesses, let us also lay aside every weight, and
sin which clings so closely, and let us run with endurance the race that is set before us, looking to Jesus, the
founder and perfecter of our faith, who for the joy that
was set before Him endured the cross, despising the
shame, and is seated at the right hand of the throne of
God. (Hebrews 12:1–2)

When the righteous cry for help, the LORD hears and delivers them out of all their troubles. The LORD is near to the brokenhearted and saves the crushed in spirit. Many are the afflictions of the righteous, but the LORD delivers him out of them all. He keeps all his bones; not one of them is broken. (Psalm 34:17–20)

And my God will supply every need of yours according to His riches in glory in Christ Jesus. (Philippians 4:19)

But He said to me, "My grace is sufficient for you, for My power is made perfect in weakness." Therefore I will boast all the more gladly of my weaknesses, so that the power of Christ may rest upon me. (2 Corinthians 12:9)

Come to Me, all who labor and are heavy laden, and I will give you rest. (Matthew 11:28)

But Jesus looked at them and said, "With man this is impossible, but with God all things are possible." (Matthew 19:26)

Tips for Leading a Small Group

The study questions at the end of the chapters can be used for individual or group study. When possible, group study is recommended. Jesus said, "For where two or three are gathered in My name, there am I among them" (Matthew 18:20). Jesus is always with us, every moment of every day. Yet in these words, He promises to be present in an extra special way when we gather together in His name.

Leading a group study is more art than science. Group conversations take on a life of their own. As a leader, your job is to facilitate the conversation, not to have all the answers. God's Word has the answers. Consider yourself a tour guide, taking participants through the book content and the Bible passages upon which each chapter is based.

Here are some tips for leading a group study. The list is not exhaustive but contains some insights gained from personal experience in leading groups.

- One goal of group study is learning. You're helping participants learn about God, faith, our world, and themselves. The Holy Spirit is our teacher. He works through God's Word, the Bible. We also learn from Spirit-filled people as they share their life experiences and wisdom in conversation.

- Another goal of group study is relationships. You're coming together to get to know one another and to grow closer. Group study is a great opportunity to build community. The discussion doesn't have to be all serious—laughter and fun help us bond with one another too.

- It's better to take your time on a single question than to rush and try to finish the list of questions. If a certain question is generating a lot of great discussion, allow the conversation to go a little longer. At some point, of course, you'll want to move on, but don't feel pressured to cover every question.

- When people choose to be vulnerable in their answers, handle those moments with care. A prior understanding of confidentiality can prevent personal information from being shared outside the group. As a group leader, you'll want to affirm people, thank them for sharing, validate their feelings, and maintain an environment in which participants feel comfortable sharing.

- Prayer is an important part of group study. We have the privilege of praying for one another, lifting up our concerns and joys to the Lord. You're encouraged to ask for prayer requests at the end of each session. As a leader, you might write prayer requests in a notebook for personal record keeping. During each session, you can follow up on the previous week's prayer requests. In many cases, the leader or a volunteer should speak all the prayer requests. If everyone in the group is comfortable praying out loud, however, you might invite everyone to pray during prayer time.

- Be careful not to allow the group to get sidetracked by personal soapboxes or political discussions. As a leader, you are the one to reel things in if the discussion gets off-topic or too heated. It's not rude—it's responsible leadership to say, "Thank you for sharing. We need to move on to the next question."

- To get a conversation off the ground, you might want to share first. Sometimes people need a moment to process a question and develop an answer. At times, participants may hesitate to be the first to speak. In those cases, you can break the ice by going first.

- Keep the discussion grounded in the Gospel. Every person in your group is a precious child of God, redeemed by the blood of Christ.

The overall tone of the discussion should be positive, uplifting, encouraging, gracious, and kind—reflecting the love that God has for us.

Acknowledgments

This book has been a team effort. Thank you to everyone who has shared guidance, input, and wisdom about the words on these pages. Your contributions have been invaluable!

Special thanks to Dr. Jerry Kieschnick for taking time out of your busy schedule to write the foreword. With your experiences in leading change at the highest level of leadership in The Lutheran Church—Missouri Synod and your extensive knowledge of the Bible, your perspective was the perfect way to begin this book.

Thank you to those who reviewed the manuscript before its submission to the publisher and gave excellent feedback: Doug Bielefeldt, Jack Goldberger, Alice Klement, Gary Larsen, and Dan Mueller.

Thank you to my wife, Ashley, for your love and encouragement throughout all the changes we've been through, including marriage, births, deaths, friends moving away, new friends being added to our lives, changing roles at church and in your work, a move to a different house, and more!

Thank you to my children for bringing so much joy into my life. Caleb, Ethan, Emma, and Zachary: You are growing up so fast! As I watch you change, I'm so grateful for the wonderful children God has given me, for who you're becoming day by day, and for your faith as it matures. "I have no greater joy than to hear that my children are walking in the truth" (3 John 4).

Thank you to Dad and Mom for always being in my corner, no matter what, and to my sister, Kelly, for likewise being a constant source of support.

Thank you to the team at Concordia Publishing House for your excellent work, especially to Laura Lane and Jamie Moldenhauer for your part in shaping the concept and content of this book.

Thank you to the wonderful people of Shepherd of the Hills Lutheran Church, School, and Child Care! Most of these chapters were originally sermons that you heard in worship. A preacher could not have a better audience for his sermons. Your love for God's Word makes the preaching task even more enjoyable.

Thanks be to God for our Savior, Jesus, who is with us in the ups and downs of life. Through every change, His steadfast love never ceases, and His mercies never come to an end!

ALSO BY
CHRISTOPHER M. KENNEDY

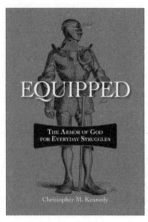

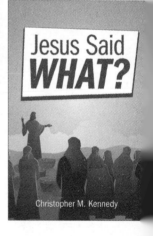

CPH.ORG